Cambridge Practice Tests for First Certificate 1

SELF-STUDY EDITION

Paul Carne
Louise Hashemi and
Barbara Thomas

CAMBRIDGE
UNIVERSITY PRESS

PUBLISHED BY THE PRESS SYNDICATE OF THE UNIVERSITY OF CAMBRIDGE
The Pitt Building, Trumpington Street, Cambridge, United Kingdom

CAMBRIDGE UNIVERSITY PRESS
The Edinburgh Building, Cambridge CB2 2RU, UK
40 West 20th Street, New York, NY 10011–4211, USA
10 Stamford Road, Oakleigh, VIC 3166, Australia
Ruiz de Alarcón 13, 28014 Madrid, Spain
Dock House, The Waterfront, Cape Town 8001, South Africa

http://www.cambridge.org

First published 1996
Eighth printing 2001

Printed in the United Kingdom at the University Press, Cambridge

ISBN 0 521 49895 3 Student's Book
ISBN 0 521 49896 1 Self-study Student's Book
ISBN 0 521 49897 X Teacher's Book
ISBN 0 521 49898 8 Class Cassette Set

Cambridge Practice Tests for First Certificate
1

Self-Study Edition

Contents

Thanks

We are grateful to Jeanne McCarten, Elizabeth Sharman, Amanda Ogden, Judith Greet and Peter Ducker of CUP for their hard work in helping us; to everyone at AVP Recording Studio and to all the people at UCLES who provided us with information.

The authors and publishers would also like to thank the teachers and students at the following institutions for piloting the material for us:

The Cheltenham School of English; The Bell Language School, Saffron Walden; The British Institute, Paris; Basil Paterson College, Edinburgh; Anglo Continental, Bournemouth; The British Institute, Florence; International House, Barcelona; Oxford House College, London.

Acknowledgements

The publishers are grateful to the following for permission to reproduce copyright material. It has not always been possible to identify sources of all the material used, and in such cases the publishers would welcome information from the copyright owners.

The Guardian/Observer for the articles on p. 35 (*Life* magazine 3.4.94) and p. 87 (*The Guardian* April 1986); New Crane Publishing Ltd for the article on p. 36 (*Sainsbury's Magazine* March 1994); Lands' End Direct Merchants UK Ltd for the article on p. 38 (October 1994 © Lands' End, Inc. All rights reserved; The Consumers' Association; Gruner+Jahr UK for the extracts from *Focus* magazine on p. 47 (January 1994), p. 49 (November 1993), p. 105 (April 1993), p. 124 (September 1994) and p. 126 (April 1993); Harrington Kilbride Publishing Group plc for the article on p. 61 (*Healthcare* Spring 1994); *The Independent* for the article on p. 62 (from 'BBC serves up a celebrity ace for Grandstand viewers by David Lister 22.2.94); Richard Ehrlich for the article on p. 64 (originally published in *She* magazine) © David Ehrlich; Phoenix Publishing and Media Limited for the article on p. 67 (*Essentially America* Summer 1994); David Higham Associates for the extract on p. 73 (from *Mr Pye* by Mervin Peake 1975); Moorland Publishing Co. Ltd for the extract on p. 79 (from *Visitor's Guide to Hampshire and the Isle of Wight* by John Barton 1990); Writers News Ltd for the article on p. 88 (*Writing* Magazine Spring 1994); BBC Worldwide Publishing for the Go wild! extract on p. 93 (*BBC Holidays* March 1994) and the article on p. 119 (*BBC Vegetarian Good Food*); The Youth Hostels Association for the Win a Fabulous Holiday extract on p. 94 (*Triangle* magazine Autumn 1993); John Boswell Associates for the extract on p. 101 (from *The Complete Book of Long-distance and Competitive Cycling* by Tom Doughty, published by Simon and Schuster 1983); Julie Davidson for the article on p. 114 (*Infusion* magazine Spring 1994), printed with the kind permission of the Tea Council); Visual Imagination Ltd for the article by Judy Sloane on p. 116 (*Film Review* No. 6); Reed Consumer Books Ltd for the extract on p. 130 (from *New Ideas for Family Meals* by Louise Steele 1988).

Photographs: Tony Stone Images (p. 39); London Stanstead Airport (p. 41); Bridgeman Art Library (p. 64); Ace Photo Agency (p. 67); Ronald Grant Archive (p. 116). Drawings by Leslie Marshall (pp. 43, 95, 120)

Colour Paper 5 Section: Photographs by J. Pembrey (1A, 2A, 2C, 2D, 4E); ZEFA (1B, 2B, 1C, 1D, 3B, 4A, 4D); N. Luckhurst (2E: T-shirt, Shakespeare book, football strip, calendar, 4B); Mirror Syndication International (2E: kilt); The Image Bank (2E: pullover, Twinings tea); John Birdsall (2F, 2G, 2H, 2I); Ace Photo (3A, 4C); Tony Stone Worldwide (3C); Rex Features (3D). Drawings by Leslie Marshall (1.5E) and Shaun Williams (3.5E).

Book design by Peter Ducker MSTD

Introduction

What is FCE?

The First Certificate in English (FCE) is an examination at intermediate level which is offered by UCLES (the University of Cambridge Local Examinations Syndicate). This book contains four practice tests which are very similar to the exam. You can use them to help you prepare for FCE. If you want more information about FCE and you cannot find it in this book, you should write to UCLES, 1 Hills Road, Cambridge CB1 2EU, England.

FCE consists of five papers, each carrying 20 per cent of the total marks.

Paper 1   Reading
You have 1 hour 15 minutes to answer the questions on the answer sheet provided. There are four parts, each containing a text and some questions. You are asked different kinds of questions in each part. There are 35 questions altogether.

Paper 2   Writing
You have 1 hour 30 minutes to write your answers on the answer sheet provided. You have to answer two questions. There is no choice in Part 1 but in Part 2 you can choose between four questions. One of these is about set books and you will only be able to answer this if you have prepared for it.

Paper 3   Use of English
You have 1 hour 15 minutes to answer the questions on the answer sheet provided. There are five different tasks which test your understanding and control of English grammar and vocabulary. There are 65 questions altogether.

Paper 4   Listening
You have 40 minutes to listen and answer the questions on the answer sheet provided. There are four parts – two parts contain long texts and the other two contain several short texts. You are asked different kinds of questions in each part. There are 30 questions altogether.

Paper 5   Speaking
The Speaking Test lasts for about 15 minutes. You take this test with another candidate. There are two examiners but only one takes part in the conversation with you. You will talk to the other candidate as well as to the examiner.

At the back of this book are examples of the answer sheets used in the exam.

When should I take the FCE exam?

If you already know something about Cambridge examinations, it is fairly easy to decide if you are ready for FCE. If you have passed the Preliminary English Test (PET), you will need about another 200 hours of active study, that is, about five hours a week for a year (either in a classroom or on your own) before you are ready to take FCE. This is an average and how long it takes you will depend on how hard you work, how quickly you learn, etc.

If you have not taken PET, look at Test 1 in this book. Try doing Paper 1 Part 2, Paper 3 Part 2 and Paper 4 Part 1. Check your answers in the Key. You need to average around 60 per cent across all five papers to be sure of passing FCE, although your score may be higher in some papers and lower in others.

Remember that FCE is not an elementary exam. If you are going to pass, you need to be fairly confident about English in all the following areas – reading, writing, listening, grammar, vocabulary and speaking. You need to be able to use and understand the main structures of English and a wide range of vocabulary and be able to communicate with English-speaking people in a range of social situations. People who pass FCE are usually considered to be ready to begin using English at work or for study.

What will I need in order to study for FCE?

You will need:
- A good English/English dictionary and a reliable modern reference grammar of English. There are excellent dictionaries and grammar reference books available which are specially written for students of English as a foreign language.
- A cassette recorder to play the cassettes which contain the listening tests. If you like music, you can use it to play songs in English on cassette and try listening to the words. Many cassettes and CDs have the words printed with them so you can look at the words while listening. You can also buy recordings of books on cassette read by famous actors.

You will find useful:
- An up-to-date translating dictionary (English/your language).
- A radio to listen to English-language programmes. For details of British overseas broadcasts, write to The BBC, Bush House, PO Box 76, The Strand, London WC2 4PH. Ask about programmes aimed at people studying English, as well as the usual programmes. It may also be possible to hear American or Australian radio stations in your area. Go to the local library or contact the local Consulates of English-speaking countries to find out.
- A video recorder so that you can watch English language films.
- English-speaking friends to practise with. Make the most of any chance to talk to people whose first language is English, but it is also very helpful to speak English with your friends. Remember most people who learn English use it to communicate with other people who are also learners.
- An English-speaking penfriend. If you cannot find a penfriend whose first language is English, try exchanging letters in English with friends who may be studying English in another town.

- Magazines, newspapers and stories in English if you can find them. There are also series of simplified readers specially written for foreign learners which will help you improve your reading and vocabulary.

How should I organise my studying?

- Be realistic. Don't plan to do more than you can, you will only disappoint yourself.
- Don't plan to give up all your free time to studying. Studying hard for one hour four times a week can be very effective. In fact, short sessions are best, because your memory won't get tired, and so you will remember what you study.
- Try to study in a quiet place so that you can concentrate well.
- Be organised. Write out a timetable and follow it. Spend a few minutes of each study period revising what you did last time.

What does this book contain?

This book is divided into four parts:

Study notes
This part goes through each paper, explaining and describing the different questions. There are suggestions about how to answer the questions and how to prepare for the exam.

Taking the exam
This part contains practical information and advice about taking the exam.

The Practice Tests
This part contains the practice papers, which are like the real ones in the exam. There are four practice tests, each one containing five papers (Reading, Writing, Use of English, Listening, Speaking) as in the exam.

The Keys and Tapescripts
This part contains all the answers to the tests and the complete tapescript for the listening papers. For Paper 2 (Writing) there are example composition answers for Test 1 and example composition plans for Tests 2, 3 and 4.

Study notes

Paper 1 Reading

- The texts on Paper 1 come from a range of English-language publications – newspapers, magazines, stories, leaflets, instructions, advertisements. Try to read as much as you can in English so you get used to texts of different kinds.
- There are always four texts. At first it may seem that there is a lot to read but, when you look at the questions, you will realise that you do not need to understand every word.
- You can get an idea of what a text is going to be about by looking at the way it is laid out on the page, the way it is printed, the headings and any illustrations. These things will all help you when you start to read the text.
- Before you begin to answer the questions, always read the instructions carefully. Each part of the test asks you to do something different so make sure you have understood **all** the instructions before you begin. This book will give you practice in the reading tasks you may meet in the exam.
- Look at the examples in Parts 1, 3 and 4 where you are shown what to do.
- If you don't understand part of a text or a particular word, try to guess by looking at the words around it, but don't spend too long on it. Leave it and come back to it later as you may find it easier to understand when you have read the rest of the text. Remember you may not even need to understand it to answer the questions.
- Practise doing the paper in the time allowed so you do not need to rush any parts in the exam.
- Practise transferring your answers to the answer sheet. In the exam, it is better to do this while you are doing the test rather than leave it till the end. If you don't do this, you might run out of time, and have no answers to hand in. If you don't know, always guess – you may be right!

Part 1

Part 1 is always a matching exercise – matching paragraphs in a text to either headings (see below) or summary sentences (e.g. Test 2 Part 1). The example below is a headings exercise. The paragraphs in the text are numbered **1–7**. There are always six or seven questions plus the example. The first paragraph is the example (**0**) and is done for you. The headings or summary sentences appear in a box before the text and each one has a letter (**A–I**). The last letter is always the answer to the example. There is always one extra heading or summary sentence which does not fit anywhere.

- Read the headings first. Then read the text through once. Now go back to the beginning and, after you have read each paragraph, try to match it with its heading. If you are not sure, leave a blank or put a question mark on your question paper.
- If you think two answers fit one question, note them both on the question paper. When you have finished, go back to the beginning and read the text again, this time choosing and checking your final answers. Then transfer them to the answer sheet.

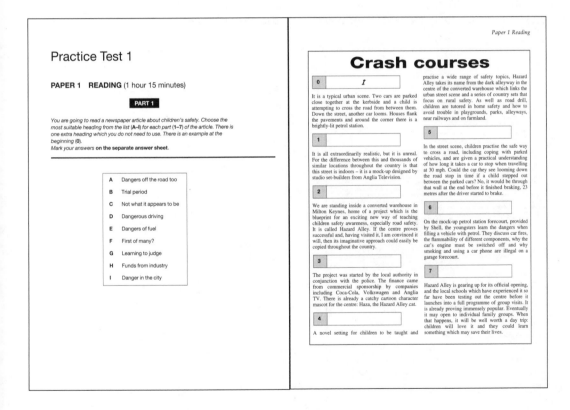

Part 2

This is always a multiple choice exercise – there are seven or eight questions which have four-choice answers. You must choose **A, B, C** or **D** as the correct answer.

- Read the text first. Try to get a general idea of what it is about. Try to understand as much as possible of the detail while you are reading but, if there are parts you do not understand, do not spend lots of time on them as they may not be tested.
- Look at the first question and find the part of the text which it refers to. Read that section again and answer the question. Only one of the choices is correct.
- Most of the questions test detailed understanding of the text but one or two test whether you understand the relation between words and phrases in one part of the text. For example, to answer question 9 below, find the word 'it' and read the text around it (several sentences) to decide exactly what it refers to.
- The questions all come in the order of the information in the text but one question (usually the last) may test your understanding of the complete text, e.g. question 15 below.
- When you have finished, transfer your answers to the answer sheet.

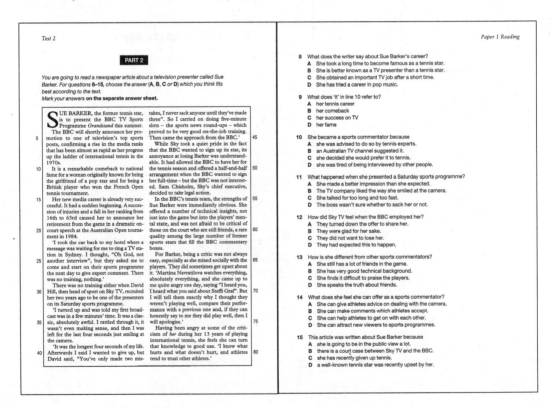

Test 2

Paper 1 Reading

PART 2

You are going to read a newspaper article about a television presenter called Sue Barker. For questions 8–15, choose the answer (A, B, C or D) which you think fits best according to the text.
Mark your answers **on the separate answer sheet.**

SUE BARKER, the former tennis star, is to present the BBC TV Sports Programme *Grandstand* this summer.
   The BBC will shortly announce her promotion to one of television's top sports posts, confirming a rise in the media ranks that has been almost as rapid as her progress up the ladder of international tennis in the 1970s.
   It is a remarkable comeback to national fame for a woman originally known for being the girlfriend of a pop star and for being a British player who won the French Open tennis tournament.
   Her new media career is already very successful. It had a sudden beginning. A succession of injuries and a fall in her ranking from 16th to 63rd caused her to announce her retirement from the game in a dramatic on-court speech at the Australian Open tournament in 1984.
   'I took the car back to my hotel where a message was waiting for me to ring a TV station in Sydney. I thought, "Oh God, not another interview", but they asked me to come and start on their sports programme the next day to give expert comment. There was no training, nothing.'
   There was no training either when David Hill, then head of sport on Sky TV, recruited her two years ago to be one of the presenters on its Saturday sports programme.
   'I turned up and was told my first broadcast was in a few minutes' time. It was a classic, absolutely awful. I rattled through it, it wasn't even making sense, and then I was left for the last four seconds just smiling at the camera.
   'It was the longest four seconds of my life. Afterwards I said I wanted to give up, but David said, "You've only made two mis-

takes, I never sack anyone until they've made three". So I carried on doing five-minute slots – the sports news round-ups – which proved to be very good on-the-job training. Then came the approach from the BBC.'
   While Sky took a quiet pride in the fact that the BBC wanted to sign up its star, its annoyance at losing Barker was understandable. It had allowed the BBC to have her for the tennis season and offered a half-and-half arrangement when the BBC wanted to sign her full-time – but the BBC was not interested. Sam Chisholm, Sky's chief executive, decided to take legal action.
   In the BBC's tennis team, the strengths of Sue Barker were immediately obvious. She offered a number of technical insights, not just into the game but into the players' mental state, and was not afraid to be critical of those on the court who are still friends, a rare quality among the large number of former sports stars that fill the BBC commentary boxes.
   For Barker, being a critic was not always easy, especially as she mixed socially with the players. They did sometimes get upset about it. 'Martina Navratilova watches everything, absolutely everything, and she came up to me quite angry one day, saying "I heard you, I heard what you said about Steffi Graf". But I will tell them exactly why I thought they weren't playing well, compare their performance with a previous one and, if they can honestly say to me they did play well, then I will apologise.'
   Having been angry at some of the criticism of *her* during her 13 years of playing international tennis, she feels she can turn that knowledge to good use. 'I know what hurts and what doesn't hurt, and athletes tend to trust other athletes.'

8   What does the writer say about Sue Barker's career?
   A   She took a long time to become famous as a tennis star.
   B   She is better known as a TV presenter than a tennis star.
   C   She obtained an important TV job after a short time.
   D   She has tried a career in pop music.

9   What does 'it' in line 10 refer to?
   A   her tennis career
   B   her comeback
   C   her success on TV
   D   her fame

10   She became a sports commentator because
   A   she was advised to do so by tennis experts.
   B   an Australian TV channel suggested it.
   C   she decided she would prefer it to tennis.
   D   she was tired of being interviewed by other people.

11   What happened when she presented a Saturday sports programme?
   A   She made a better impression than she expected.
   B   The TV company liked the way she smiled at the camera.
   C   She talked for too long and too fast.
   D   The boss wasn't sure whether to sack her or not.

12   How did Sky TV feel when the BBC employed her?
   A   They turned down the offer to share her.
   B   They were glad for her sake.
   C   They did not want to lose her.
   D   They had expected this to happen.

13   How is she different from other sports commentators?
   A   She still has a lot of friends in the game.
   B   She has very good technical background.
   C   She finds it difficult to praise the players.
   D   She speaks the truth about friends.

14   What does she feel she can offer as a sports commentator?
   A   She can give athletes advice on dealing with the camera.
   B   She can make comments which athletes accept.
   C   She can help athletes to get on with each other.
   D   She can attract new viewers to sports programmes.

15   This article was written about Sue Barker because
   A   she is going to be in the public view a lot.
   B   there is a court case between Sky TV and the BBC.
   C   she has recently given up tennis.
   D   a well-known tennis star was recently upset by her.

Part 3

This is always a gapped text – either gapped sentences or gapped paragraphs.

There are six or seven questions plus an example. In a gapped sentence exercise, one sentence has been removed from every paragraph of a text and you have to fit them back where they belong (e.g. Test 3 Part 3).

In a gapped paragraph exercise, a number of paragraphs have been removed from a text and you have to fit them back where they belong (see below).

The sentences or paragraphs which have been removed are in a box which comes after the text. Each gap in the text has a number (**1, 2, 3,** etc.) and each sentence/paragraph in the box has a letter (**A, B, C,** etc.). The first gap in the text is labelled **0** and is the example, so it is done for you. There is one extra sentence/paragraph in the box, which does not fit anywhere.

- Read through the main text to get a general idea of what it is saying.
- Then read the sentences/paragraphs in the box. Notice anything about them which makes them different from each other, e.g. some may be in the past tense, some in the present tense.
- Go back to the text and look at the first gap. Look at the sentences before and after the gap and decide what information is needed to join them together. Now look at the sentences/paragraphs in the box again and try to find the one which fits. If you can't decide, leave that one and come back to it later as some of the other gaps may be easier.
- When you are happy with your answers, transfer them to the answer sheet.

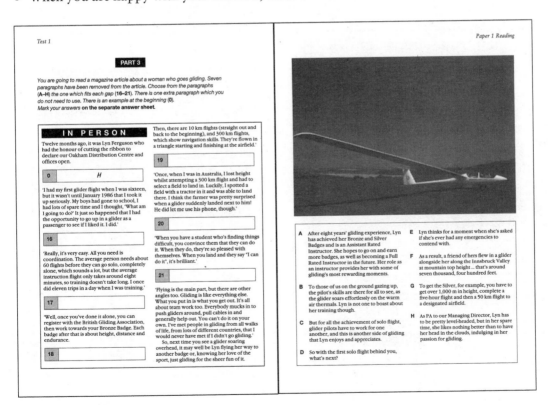

Part 4

This is always a multiple matching exercise with between 13 and 15 questions. You are asked to find different pieces of information in the text. There may also be a multiple choice question at the end which tests your understanding of the text as a whole. Part 4 may look harder than some of the other parts of the paper because there are so many questions but they are usually quicker to do than multiple choice or gapped text questions. The text may also look long but you do not usually need to understand every word.

- Read the questions first and then look through the text trying to find the answers. You do not need to understand every word. When you have found the answer, note it down. If you are unsure, put a question mark beside it so that you can go back and check it later when you have done the other questions and know the text better.
- Transfer your answers to the answer sheet.

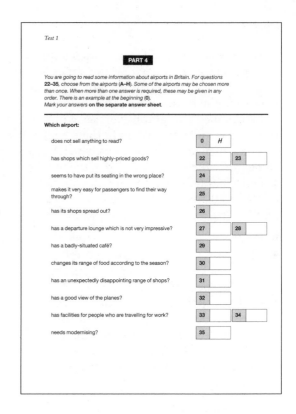

Test 1

PART 4

You are going to read some information about airports in Britain. For questions 22–35, choose from the airports (**A–H**). Some of the airports may be chosen more than once. When more than one answer is required, these may be given in any order. There is an example at the beginning (**0**).
Mark your answers **on the separate answer sheet.**

Which airport:

does not sell anything to read?	**0** *H*	
has shops which sell highly-priced goods?	**22**	**23**
seems to have put its seating in the wrong place?	**24**	
makes it very easy for passengers to find their way through?	**25**	
has its shops spread out?	**26**	
has a departure lounge which is not very impressive?	**27**	**28**
has a badly-situated café?	**29**	
changes its range of food according to the season?	**30**	
has an unexpectedly disappointing range of shops?	**31**	
has a good view of the planes?	**32**	
has facilities for people who are travelling for work?	**33**	**34**
needs modernising?	**35**	

Paper 1 Reading

Which airport?

The choice of where to fly from has never been greater, particularly for those flying on a package holiday. For each airport, we looked at the facilities (e.g. restaurants, waiting areas, etc.) offered before going through passport control (land-side) and after going through passport control (air-side).

A   Heathrow 4

The check-in hall is spacious and modern. There are few land-side shops but the essentials are available. A café with pine seating and a medium range of hot dishes and salads is situated upstairs. There are more facilities air-side. The shops are clustered into the central part of the 500-metre long hall, and expensive ranges are well represented. There's plenty of natural light from the windows that overlook the runway and lots of seating away from the shopping area.

B   Manchester 2

The check-in hall has a high glass roof which lets in natural light. The café is at one end and slightly separated from the rest of the facilities, which makes it much more pleasant. There's also an up-market coffee shop. Hundreds of seats – little used when we visited despite the passengers crowded below – are available upstairs. The departure lounge is bright and has plenty of space, the cafeteria is pleasant.

C   Stansted

Passengers can walk in a straight line from the entrance, through the check-in to the monorail that takes them to their plane. Land-side, ➤➤

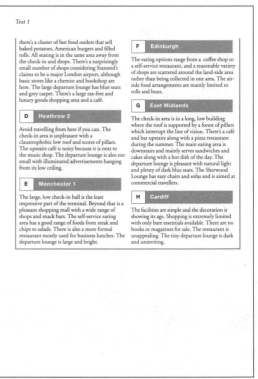

Test 1

there's a cluster of fast food outlets that sell baked potatoes, American burgers and filled rolls. All seating is in the same area away from the check-in and shops. There's a surprisingly small number of shops considering Stansted's claims to be a major London airport, although basic stores like a chemist and bookshop are here. The large departure lounge has blue seats and grey carpet. There's a large tax-free and luxury goods shopping area and a café.

D   Heathrow 2

Avoid travelling from here if you can. The check-in area is unpleasant with a claustrophobic low roof and scores of pillars. The upstairs café is noisy because it is next to the music shop. The departure lounge is also too small with illuminated advertisements hanging from its low ceiling.

E   Manchester 1

The large, low check-in hall is the least impressive part of the terminal. Beyond that is a pleasant shopping mall with a wide range of shops and snack bars. The self-service eating area has a good range of foods from steak and chips to salads. There is also a more formal restaurant mostly used for business lunches. The departure lounge is large and bright.

F   Edinburgh

The eating options range from a coffee shop to a self-service restaurant, and a reasonable variety of shops are scattered around the land-side area rather than being collected in one area. The air-side food arrangements are mainly limited to rolls and buns.

G   East Midlands

The check-in area is in a long, low building where the roof is supported by a forest of pillars which interrupt the line of vision. There's a café and bar upstairs along with a pizza restaurant during the summer. The main eating area is downstairs and mainly serves sandwiches and cakes along with a hot dish of the day. The departure lounge is pleasant with natural light and plenty of dark blue seats. The Sherwood Lounge has easy chairs and sofas and is aimed at commercial travellers.

H   Cardiff

The facilities are simple and the decoration is showing its age. Shopping is extremely limited with only bare essentials available. There are no books or magazines for sale. The restaurant is unappealing. The tiny departure lounge is dark and uninviting.

Paper 2 Writing

- Each of your answers must be between 120 and 180 words. The exact number is **not** important. The best thing to do is to measure your handwriting when you are preparing for the exam, so that you know what 120 and 180 words in your writing look like. Once you know, you can avoid wasting valuable time counting words during the actual exam.

- The examiners do not expect your work to be perfect. Even the best students make some mistakes when they write. However, you want to make as few as possible. While you are practising for the exam, it may help you to know that you can lose marks for the following:

  - including inappropriate details (especially in Part 1)
  - using material from the exam paper without adapting it to fit what you are writing (especially in Part 1)
  - leaving out important information
  - work which is not clearly organised (for example, giving information in the wrong order)
  - incorrect style (for example, writing a job application as if you were talking to a friend)
  - incorrect grammar (especially repeated mistakes or mistakes that affect meaning such as verb tenses)
  - bad spelling
  - bad punctuation
  - bad paragraphing
  - illegible handwriting

Try to set out your work tidily. If you need to change what you have written, cross out the wrong words with a single line. Do not use brackets ( ) for this.

Part 1

In Part 1, there is no choice. Everyone has to do the same task, and it is always a letter. It will not be a very formal business letter, but if it is addressed to someone you do not know very well, or a stranger, it should not sound like a letter to a friend. On the exam paper you will see up to three short texts such as advertisements, letters, notes, leaflets, diaries, timetables, notices. These texts contain all the information you need for your letter. You must read the instructions and these texts very carefully.

- Check **who** you have to write to, **why** you are writing and **what** you must include. This will help you to choose the right style, include everything you should, and avoid adding unnecessary information. You can add ideas of your own as well, provided they fit sensibly with those in the text. It is useful to mark the exam paper with a pen or highlighter so that you can see which information is important.

- Then you should make a short plan (see example on page 138). This is very important. If you have already put your ideas in order before you begin to write, you can think carefully about your language and avoid mistakes.

- It is not a good idea to copy out whole sentences from the texts on the question paper. Of course, you may need to use some of the same words and phrases, but you must take care that they fit the meaning, and grammar of what you are writing (see model answer on page 138).

- You do not have to include any addresses, but you should begin and end in a suitable way.

PAPER 2 WRITING (1 hour 30 minutes)

PART 1

*You **must** answer this question.*

1 You are interested in attending a language course in England next summer. You have seen the advertisement below. You have also talked to your English teacher and she has suggested some things that you should check before you register.

Read the advertisement below, together with your teacher's note. Then write to the language school, asking for information about the points mentioned by your teacher, and anything else that you think is important.

SUMMER LANGUAGE COURSES

2 weeks, 3 weeks, 1 month

Beautiful English market town. Full sports and social programme. Accommodation with friendly English families. Helpful teachers. Small classes.

Full details from: Ian Lawrence, The Smart School of English, High Street, Little Bonnington

It's a great idea for you to do a language course in England. Be careful to choose a good school. When you write, ask about these things:
– student numbers, ages
– details of sports programme etc.
– local facilities
– teachers' qualifications
Let me know if you need any more help. Good luck!

Write **a letter** of between **120–180** words in an appropriate style on the next page. Do not write any addresses.

Part 2

In Part 2, there are five tasks, from which you choose **only one**. The two choices in question 5 are related to the set books (see below). Do not attempt to answer the set book questions in the exam if you have not prepared for them. The other tasks always include at least one letter, report or application and at least one description or story or discussion.

- In every case you are told **what** to write (letter, story, etc.) and for **whom** you are writing, but in this part, it is up to you to decide on the details of the contents. Be careful to follow the instructions exactly. If you are given words for the beginning of a story, do not change them, or put them in the middle! If you are asked to write a report, this does not have to be a very formal business report. Just make sure that you think carefully about who is going to read it and what they want to learn from it. Include only the sort of information and opinions that are asked for.

PART 2

Write an answer to **one** of the questions 2–5 in this part. Write your answer in **120–180** words in an appropriate style on the next page, putting the question number in the box.

2 An international young people's magazine is investigating the question: **Do young people today really know what they want from life?**

Write a short **article** for this magazine on this topic based on your own experience.

3 You have decided to enter this competition.

Exciting chance for writers!

Write a short story and win a Great Prize

Your entry must begin or end with the following words:

No matter what people said about Alex, I knew he was a true friend.

Write your **story** for the competition.

4 You are attending a summer language course and have been asked to report on a local leisure facility (e.g. cinema, sports hall, etc) for the benefit of students attending the next course.

Write your **report** describing the facility and what it has to offer, and commenting on its good and bad points.

5 **Background reading texts**

Answer **one** of the following two questions based on your reading of **one** of the set books (see p.2). Write the title of the book next to the question number box.

Either **(a)** Describe your favourite character in the book and explain what you like about him/her.

or **(b)** Explain how the physical setting of the book is important to the success of the story.

The tasks are always different in Parts 1 and 2, so even if you write two letters, they will be quite different types.

- Again, it is very important to make a plan. As well as helping you to write correct English, it will also allow you to discover in time if you have chosen the wrong task for you. For example, you may realise that you do not remember some essential vocabulary, or that you do not have enough ideas to write about. You can quickly choose another one before you have wasted too much time.

Using the Practice Tests for Paper 2

In the Key, you will find plans for the Part 1 and Part 2 tasks of Practice Test 1. These are to help you judge the sort of thing you should write and how to organise it.

First stage (Practice Test 1)

- check exactly what you have to do (**who** are you writing to? **why** are you writing?)
- mark the important parts of the task
- write a plan
- compare your plan with the one in the Key
- make any changes you want to (remember, your plan may work just as well, so only make changes if there is a clear need to do so)
- write your answer (try to do this in about 30 minutes)
- read your answer through carefully, looking for mistakes
- compare your answer with the model – what can you learn from it? (remember, your answer may be very good, even though it is not the same)

Second stage (Practice Tests 2, 3 and 4)

- check exactly what you have to do
- mark the important parts of the task
- write a plan
- write your answer (try to do this in about 30 minutes)
- read your answer through carefully, looking for mistakes
- (for Part 1) compare your answer with the plan in the Key – what can you learn from it? (remember, your answer may be very good, even though it is not the same)

The set book questions

In Part 2 of Paper 2, there is a pair of questions about set books. If you have read any of the set books, you may choose to do **one** of these **instead of** the other questions in Part 2. The books change every two years. To find out which titles are set when you are taking the exam, look in the regulations booklet or write to UCLES (see page 1).

You do not have to read the set books, but it can be a good idea to do so. There are several reasons for this:

- Reading will help your English in general.

- It increases your choices in Paper 2 Part 2, especially if you read more than one of the books.
- It allows you to write about a subject which you know well.

Preparation

If you study the questions about set books in this book, you will see that they are always general questions which can be answered about any of the books.

- Practise describing and giving your opinion about the characters, events and settings of the books.
- Plan and check your work just as with other writing tasks.
- Do not worry about giving correct 'literary' opinions. The examiners who mark your paper are not really concerned about how clever your ideas are. They want to know how well you can use the English language to express yourself.
- Make sure that you really know the book well, so that you can answer any question about it.
- Do **not** prepare 'perfect' answers and try to fit them to any question. Examiners are very strict if they think they are marking an inappropriate answer which has been 'prepared' before the exam.

Paper 3 Use of English

- Try to spend approximately the same amount of time on each part of the paper, with probably a little more on Part 3, and a little less on Part 5. It is also important to allow enough time to check your answers, and your answer sheet, carefully.
- If you have large, and/or untidy, handwriting, you will need to be very careful when completing the answer sheet, especially in Part 3. Be very careful with your spelling in all parts of the paper.
- When the task is based on a text (Parts 1, 2, 4 and 5), read quickly through the text before you try to answer any of the questions. Don't miss out the 'example' sentences at the beginning, which will help you to get a quick general idea of what the text is about.
- The texts for Paper 3 are not as long, or as complicated, as the texts in the Reading Paper, but you should still read them carefully, to avoid losing marks through misunderstanding.
- **Parts 1, 2, 3** and **5** are all gap-filling exercises and have many similarities in the way you should work on them. Remember these points:
  - Most of the information which will help you to make the correct answer will be in the areas immediately before **or after** the gap. Everyone looks before the gap, but lots of students miss what comes after (e.g. *interested* is usually followed by *in* and so it wouldn't be a good choice as an answer to '(**18**) … for').
  - If you have a problem with some of the questions on a text, try not to waste time. Go on and do the easier questions, and come back to the difficult ones later. It's often simpler to find an answer when you have completed most of the text.
  - If you have time, it is a good idea to read through the completed text to

make sure that all your answers make sense. A few answers may be affected by ideas which are not close to the gap, and you might miss these when you are working question by question. If you do not have time to check like this when you start preparing for the exam, then you should try to improve your working speed gradually.

Part 1

Part 1 is a text of around 200 words with fifteen gaps in it. You have to choose the correct answer from four options to fill each of the gaps. The questions test mainly vocabulary.

- In most of the questions, you have to choose the only answer with the correct meaning for the gap. In a few questions, however, two or more choices may have the right meaning, and you will have to choose the only one that fits the grammar of the text.
- Some of the questions are based on fixed phrases, so it is a good idea to make a careful note of these as you meet them in your reading.

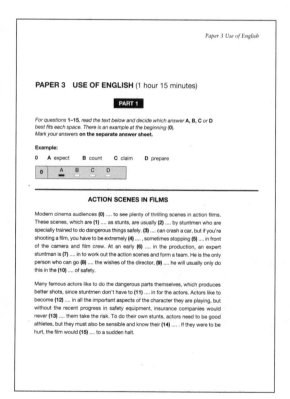

Paper 3 Use of English

PAPER 3   USE OF ENGLISH (1 hour 15 minutes)

PART 1

*For questions 1–15, read the text below and decide which answer **A, B, C or D** best fits each space. There is an example at the beginning (0).*
*Mark your answers **on the separate answer sheet**.*

Example:

0   A expect   B count   C claim   D prepare

0	A	B	C	D

ACTION SCENES IN FILMS

Modern cinema audiences **(0)** .... to see plenty of thrilling scenes in action films. These scenes, which are **(1)** .... as stunts, are usually **(2)** .... by stuntmen who are specially trained to do dangerous things safely. **(3)** .... can crash a car, but if you're shooting a film, you have to be extremely **(4)** .... , sometimes stopping **(5)** .... in front of the camera and film crew. At an early **(6)** .... in the production, an expert stuntman is **(7)** .... in to work out the action scenes and form a team. He is the only person who can go **(8)** .... the wishes of the director, **(9)** .... he will usually only do this in the **(10)** .... of safety.

Many famous actors like to do the dangerous parts themselves, which produces better shots, since stuntmen don't have to **(11)** .... in for the actors. Actors like to become **(12)** .... in all the important aspects of the character they are playing, but without the recent progress in safety equipment, insurance companies would never **(13)** .... them take the risk. To do their own stunts, actors need to be good athletes, but they must also be sensible and know their **(14)** ..... . If they were to be hurt, the film would **(15)** .... to a sudden halt.

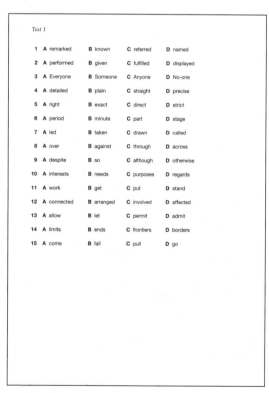

Test 1

1	A remarked	B known	C referred	D named
2	A performed	B given	C fulfilled	D displayed
3	A Everyone	B Someone	C Anyone	D No-one
4	A detailed	B plain	C straight	D precise
5	A right	B exact	C direct	D strict
6	A period	B minute	C part	D stage
7	A led	B taken	C drawn	D called
8	A over	B against	C through	D across
9	A despite	B so	C although	D otherwise
10	A interests	B needs	C purposes	D regards
11	A work	B get	C put	D stand
12	A connected	B arranged	C involved	D affected
13	A allow	B let	C permit	D admit
14	A limits	B ends	C frontiers	D borders
15	A come	B fall	C pull	D go

Part 2

Part 2 is also a text of around 200 words with fifteen gaps in it. This time you have to decide on the best word to fill each gap for yourself: there are no options to choose from. You must use **only one word** in each gap. For example, *close to* may have the correct meaning to fill a particular gap, but has too many words: *near* would be the correct choice. These questions concentrate on your knowledge of English grammar, and the words you need to fill the gaps will be quite familiar.

- When you have finished, be careful to check, for example, that singulars and plurals match up correctly, that all the verb tenses work properly, and that longer sentences are properly connected, and have a clear meaning.
- If you have trouble with a gap, try to decide what part of speech you need (e.g. noun, verb, pronoun, etc.), so that you can see how the sentence works. This may help with the next question, even if you don't find the exact word. Some questions may have more than one correct answer, but these will usually have the same meaning (e.g. *each/every*; *because/as/since*). You will get to know most of these groups as you practise for the examination. Above all, try not to waste time choosing the best of two or three equally correct answers.

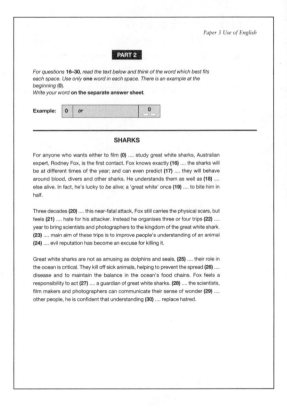

Paper 3 Use of English

PART 2

For questions **16–30**, *read the text below and think of the word which best fits each space. Use only* **one** *word in each space. There is an example at the beginning* **(0)**.
Write your word **on the separate answer sheet.**

Example: | 0 | *or* | | 0 |

SHARKS

For anyone who wants either to film **(0)** .... study great white sharks, Australian expert, Rodney Fox, is the first contact. Fox knows exactly **(16)** .... the sharks will be at different times of the year; and can even predict **(17)** .... they will behave around blood, divers and other sharks. He understands them as well as **(18)** .... else alive. In fact, he's lucky to *be* alive; a 'great white' once **(19)** .... to bite him in half.

Three decades **(20)** .... this near-fatal attack, Fox still carries the physical scars, but feels **(21)** .... hate for his attacker. Instead he organises three or four trips **(22)** .... year to bring scientists and photographers to the kingdom of the great white shark. **(23)** .... main aim of these trips is to improve people's understanding of an animal **(24)** .... evil reputation has become an excuse for killing it.

Great white sharks are not as amusing as dolphins and seals, **(25)** .... their role in the ocean is critical. They kill off sick animals, helping to prevent the spread **(26)** .... disease and to maintain the balance in the ocean's food chains. Fox feels a responsibility to act **(27)** .... a guardian of great white sharks. **(28)** .... the scientists, film makers and photographers can communicate their sense of wonder **(29)** .... other people, he is confident that understanding **(30)** .... replace hatred.

Part 3

Part 3 consists of ten separate questions, which test both grammar and vocabulary. You have to complete a gap in a sentence so that it means the same as the sentence printed above it. You are given one 'key' word which you must use as part of the answer. You must not change this word in any way, and your answer must contain **a minimum of two words and a maximum of five,** including the key word. As in Part 2, you may be able to think of a longer way of filling the gap with correct English, but **answers of six words and more will lose marks,** so you must follow the rules very carefully.

- Read the original sentence very carefully, and notice which parts of the meaning are missing from the new sentence (your answer must not lose any important parts of the meaning of the original sentence). Then, look at the key word and think what else will be necessary when you fit it into the gap, perhaps a verb or noun will need to be followed by a particular preposition, or an infinitive may need other suitable words to form the correct tense. Be especially careful if the key word could be two different parts of speech (e.g. *help* – noun and verb; *good* – adjective and noun), since it is likely that only one of these will make a successful answer.
- It is fine to use **short forms** (e.g. *you're, won't, we've, they'd,* etc.) in your answers, but **you must count them as two words,** since that is what they represent (e.g. *you are, will not, we have, they would,* etc.). Apostrophes ('), of course, can also show possession – in phrases like *David's house, the policeman's car* etc. In this case, *David's* and *policeman's* count as **one word** each.

- Do not change any vocabulary from the original sentence unless the question forces you to do this. It may seem safe to change *able* to *capable*, even though you do not have to, but there is no point in doing this, and it may lead to other problems which you haven't noticed.
- Check that your answer does not unnecessarily repeat ideas which are already in the new sentence, and remember: answers which change the key word in any way or use too many words will lose marks.
- As you work through the Practice Tests, notice the points which are commonly tested, so that you have an idea of what to expect in the examination. When you are studying grammar, look out for any exercises which ask you to express the same idea in different ways.

Test 1

PART 3

*For questions **31–40**, complete the second sentence so that it has a similar meaning to the first sentence, using the word given. **Do not change the word given**. You must use between two and five words, including the word given. There is an example at the beginning (0).*
*Write **only** the missing words **on the separate answer sheet**.*

Example:

0 I last saw him at my 21st birthday party.
   since

   I .... my 21st birthday party.

The gap can be filled by the words 'haven't seen him since' so you write:

| **0** | *haven't seen him since* | **0** | **0** | **1** | **2** |

31 'You've broken my radio, Frank!' said Jane.
   accused

   Jane .... her radio.

32 My car really needs to be repaired soon.
   must

   I really .... repaired soon.

33 Susan regrets not buying that house.
   wishes

   Susan .... that house.

34 I could never have succeeded without your help.
   you

   I could never have succeeded .... me.

35 I thought I might run out of cash, so I took my cheque-book with me.
   case

   I took my cheque-book with me .... out of cash.

36 Linda's plans for a picnic have been spoilt by the weather.
   fallen

   Linda's plans for a picnic .... because of the weather.

37 The bread was too stale to eat.
   fresh

   The bread .... to eat.

38 Perhaps Brian went home early.
   may

   Brian .... home early.

39 I can't possibly work in all this noise!
   impossible

   It .... work in all this noise!

40 The thief suddenly realised that the police were watching him.
   watched

   The thief suddenly realised that he .... by the police.

Part 4

Part 4 is a text of about 200 words with mistakes in most of the lines. You have to tick (✓) correct lines and for incorrect lines, you must write the *extra and unnecessary* word which makes the line incorrect in the space provided on your answer sheet. This exercise tests your ability to notice a variety of errors in a piece of connected English.

- Although not all the mistakes will be the type you make in your own writing, practising checking English for errors will help you in your own work for the Writing paper. If you have the opportunity, exchange written work with a friend. This can provide variety, and it is often easier to learn to notice mistakes in someone else's work, rather than your own.

- Between three and five of the fifteen tested lines will be correct. The extra words which you must find are always clearly inappropriate, not just words which can be left out, and these errors may appear anywhere in the line. This means that a word early in the line may be wrong because of something in the line above; a word near the end may be wrong because of what follows on the next line. For this reason, it is important to remember that you are working on a **complete** text, and not fifteen separate questions.

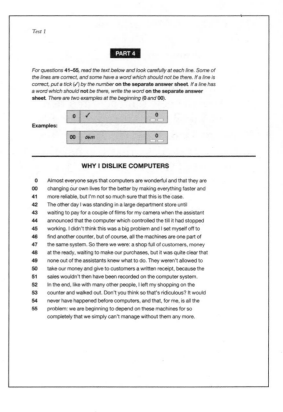

Part 5

Part 5 is a text of about 150 words with ten gaps in it. You have to fill the gaps by forming suitable parts of speech from the words given in capitals at the side of each line. You may, for example, have to turn a verb into a noun (e.g. *appear → appearance*), a noun into an adverb (e.g. *success → successfully*) etc. These questions test your ability to decide which part of speech is needed and to form the correct answer.

- You may have to think about other ideas in the text to find the right answer. For example, whether a person in a text is *fortunate* or *unfortunate* may depend on ideas which are some distance from the gap you are working on.
- When you have to form a noun, check the text carefully to see whether you need a singular or plural. If you write *argument*, and the text needs *arguments*, you will not get a mark.

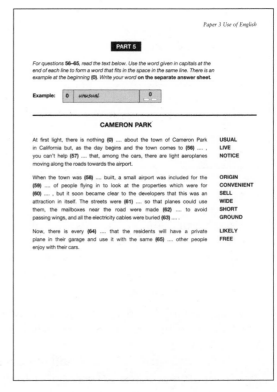

- No correct answer will involve making more than two changes to the original word given (e.g. *interest* → **uninterested** may be included, *interest* → **uninterestedly** will not be).
- If you have not taken an interest in word groups so far, now is the time to start. You may need to change the way you collect and store your vocabulary. When looking up new words in the dictionary, it is worth taking a little extra time to note down the noun that goes with a new verb and so on. You can also find useful exercises on prefixes and suffixes in many intermediate grammar books.

Paper 4 Listening

- The best preparation for the Listening paper is listening to a wide variety of spoken English. You should listen to English as often as you can, in any form available, both in school and outside. If you are not in an English-speaking country, try to get information about English language broadcasts on the radio or television. You should also look out for recorded material such as audio cassettes of songs and videos of films in English. It does not matter whether these use British or American English or what sort of accents the speakers have. The important thing is to get used to listening to spoken English. Some of the accents in the FCE examination are not standard British English, although they will never be very strong.
- Remember that these Practice Tests are at the level of difficulty of the exam. Do not start using them too early, or you may be discouraged because they seem difficult. Wait until you have had lots of listening practice with other materials and then use these Practice Tests to help you get to know what it is like to do the Listening paper.
- When you are using these Practice Tests, it is better to practise as if you were in an exam. Do not keep stopping and rewinding the tape while you are trying to answer the questions. Get used to doing each whole test without interruptions because this is what you will have to do in the exam. After you've completed and marked your test using the Key, then is the time to listen again, and look at the tapescript if you like, to help with the questions that gave you problems.
- At the end of the test you have five minutes to copy your answers onto the answer sheet. It is very important to do this carefully, checking that you do not put any answers next to the wrong question number. Also be sure you do not leave any blanks. You cannot score marks for a blank space, but a guess may be correct.

Part 1

In Part 1 there are eight questions. For each one, you hear one or two people talking for about thirty seconds. You hear this twice and have to choose the best answer **A**, **B** or **C**. The questions are read out on the tape as well, so you will not lose your place.

- Practise using the questions to help you. Do not worry about understanding every word, just listen for the information you need. Sometimes you need understand only the words used. At other times a tone of voice or emphasis may be just as important.

- Be careful with those questions in which people develop an idea or change their minds as they speak.

Test 1

PAPER 4   LISTENING (approximately 40 minutes)

PART 1

You will hear people talking in eight different situations.
For questions 1–8, choose the best answer A, B or C.

1   You are visiting a museum when you hear this man addressing a group of people.
Who is he?

   A a security guard

   B a tourist guide   **1**

   C a museum guide

2   You're in a restaurant when you overhear one of the waiters talking.
Who is he talking about?

   A a colleague

   B the manager   **2**

   C a customer

3   You're waiting in a hospital corridor when you hear this woman talking.
What does she say about her doctor?

   A He's made a mistake.

   B He's been unhelpful.   **3**

   C He's been untruthful.

4   You are out shopping when you hear a shop assistant talking to a customer.
What is she refusing to do?

   A give him some money

   B change a faulty item   **4**

   C repair something

Part 2

In Part 2 you hear one or two people talking for about three minutes. You have to answer ten questions by writing one or a few words. You **never** have to write a whole sentence. You have time to read through the questions before the piece begins, there is a short pause after you hear it and then it is repeated.

- You can write your answers at any time. Spelling mistakes do not lose marks, as long as the examiners can understand what you mean.
- Read the questions carefully because they will help you to understand what you hear. For example, in question 9 you can think about reasons for doing a holiday job. It could be because you need money, or because it helps with something you are studying, or because it might be useful for your career. If you have thought about possible answers, it will be easier to spot the correct one when you are listening.

Test 1

PART 2

You will hear a student called Bill talking about his holiday job.
For questions 9–18, complete the notes which summarise what he says. You will need to write a word or a short phrase in the box.

Reason for doing job:	**9**
Building used to be a	**10**
Good position because it's near	**11**
Main alteration: owner has added	**12**
Bill's favourite task:	**13**
Owner is very careful about	**14**
Attitude of male residents to staff:	**15**
Problem with woman who thought he was	**16**
Other staff treated Bill as	**17**
Bill is going back in order to	**18**

Part 3

In Part 3 there are five questions. You hear five pieces of speech, each about thirty seconds in length. On your question paper there is a list of six possible answers which you must match against the five pieces you hear. The group of five pieces is repeated.

- Again, use the questions to help you. Notice whether the questions are about **what** the speakers say, **who** they are, **how** they feel, etc., because you will need to listen for different types of clue in each case.
- Use the first listening to form a general idea of the answers, but try to keep an open mind until you have heard all the speakers once.
- Note your answers and then use the second listening to check them.

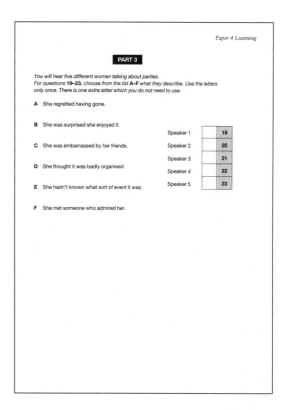

Paper 4 Listening

PART 3

You will hear five different women talking about parties.
For questions **19–23**, choose from the list **A–F** what they describe. Use the letters only once. There is one extra letter which you do not need to use.

A   She regretted having gone.

B   She was surprised she enjoyed it.

C   She was embarrassed by her friends.

D   She thought it was badly organised.

E   She hadn't known what sort of event it was.

F   She met someone who admired her.

Speaker 1	19
Speaker 2	20
Speaker 3	21
Speaker 4	22
Speaker 5	23

Part 4

Part 4 is usually a conversation, about three minutes in length. There are seven questions. These may be 'choose the best answer **A**, **B** or **C**' or some other type, such as True/False. You only have to write a letter for each answer. There is time to read the questions through before you listen to the conversation, a short pause after you hear it, and then it is repeated.

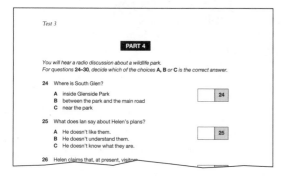

Test 3

PART 4

You will hear a radio discussion about a wildlife park.
For questions **24–30**, decide which of the choices **A, B** or **C** is the correct answer.

24   Where is South Glen?

   A   inside Glenside Park
   B   between the park and the main road
   C   near the park   24

25   What does Ian say about Helen's plans?

   A   He doesn't like them.
   B   He doesn't understand them.
   C   He doesn't know what they are.   25

26   Helen claims that, at present, visitors

Test 1

PART 4

You will hear a conversation between two teenagers, Nick and Sandra.
For questions **24–30**, decide which statements are true or false and mark your answers **T** for True or **F** for False.

24   Sandra had to do some housework before coming out.   24

25   Sandra envies Nick.   25

26   Sandra is angry with her mother.   26

27   Sandra has failed her exams.   27

- The questions usually contain lots of helpful information about how the conversation develops, so read them carefully to get an idea of what you're going to hear.

- Be careful not to choose your answers too quickly. Speakers may appear to be saying one thing at the beginning of a speech and then change direction (e.g. *I'd like to come out this evening ... but I've got too much homework.*).
- Sentences with linking words (like *but, although, if*) can cause you problems because speakers don't usually emphasise these words. If you miss the linking word, you may get the wrong idea, so make sure you know all the common linking words and can recognise them easily. Be especially careful with words which sound similar, such as *so/though, why/while, also/although*.

Paper 5 Speaking

About the Speaking paper

The Speaking paper is your chance to show how well you can use spoken English to give and exchange information and opinions. You will be examined with a partner, as this allows the examiners to test more skills than they could in a one-to-one conversation with you. There are two examiners: an *interlocutor*, who explains the tasks and asks the questions, and an *assessor*, who does not take part in the conversation, but concentrates on giving marks for what you say.

The Speaking paper lasts approximately fifteen minutes and is divided into four parts. You need to use your English in different ways, from simply talking about yourself at the start to working on particular tasks in the later parts of the paper, when you have to discuss problems with your partner and try to reach agreement.

- You will get good marks if you:
  - work well with your partner to carry out the tasks correctly
  - speak with clear pronunciation
  - speak with reasonably natural speed and rhythm
  - use a variety of grammar
  - use a variety of appropriate vocabulary.

- When you look at a list like this, it is important to remember that First Certificate is an intermediate examination. The examiners do not expect you to sound exactly like someone whose first language is English, or to have perfect grammar. You should always think about what you are saying, but don't let the fear of making mistakes prevent you from speaking freely.

Study notes

The timings below are for all the work in each part of the paper. Part 1, for instance, includes your turn, your partner's turn and the examiner's instructions to both of you. You personally will probably not speak for much more than one minute out of the four minutes allowed for this part.

Part 1

Part 1 (about four minutes) gives you the chance to get used to your partner and the examiners while you talk about familiar topics like your personal background, interests, etc. Each student has a separate turn. This part of the paper tests mainly social language.

- Be ready to talk in this part, even if you are naturally a quiet person. If the examiner asks you what you do in your free time, for instance, don't just say that you 'go out with friends'. If you do, you may not make any mistakes, but you will not show the examiner much about your English, either. *Where do you go? What do you do? Why do you enjoy it?* Talking about any of these will make you use different grammar and more vocabulary. Remember that the idea of the paper is to show what you can do, not to hide your English away so no one can criticise.

Part 2

In Part 2 (about four minutes), the examiner will give you two colour photos and ask you to talk about the photos and ideas connected with them. You can talk generally or about your own experience of the topic, if you have any. Your partner will also have a pair of pictures to talk about. This part of the paper tests your ability to give information and to express opinions.

- It will normally be useful to mention what the pictures show, but don't fall into the trap of just listing all the details you can see in the picture. If you do this, there is a chance that what you actually say will be very simple and that you will use the same grammar over and over again (*There is …; There are …; I can see …*). You wouldn't do this in your own language, and, if you prepare wisely for the examination, there is no reason for you to do it in English.
- When you first see the pictures, think why the examiners have put them together. For example, a picture of a man in a garden reading a book, together with a photo of a woman water-skiing might show two different ways of relaxing: *Which do you think is better?* or *Do you like both for different reasons?* etc. Points like these develop the conversation in a natural way and will give you a good idea of what questions the examiner might ask you. It's probably not very important in this case whether the man is wearing glasses or not and, if you talk about such small details, you may never even reach the main point of the two photos. You will also have no idea what the examiner will ask you afterwards.
- Listen carefully to everything your partner says in Parts 1 and 2. There may be an opportunity to ask a question or comment on what they say, but more importantly, you need to get used to how they speak (speed, accent, type of vocabulary, etc.) before you start working with them in Part 3. Even if you already know the person, they may be nervous or be 'putting on a show' and this may change the way they speak. You can judge whether, in Parts 3 and 4, you might need to interrupt them politely (if they are excited and can't stop talking) or ask them to repeat something (if they speak quietly or you don't understand). Turn situations like these to your advantage by learning and using appropriate expressions: for example, *I'm sorry, could you say that again?* makes a much better impression on the examiners than *What?* or *What did you say?*

Part 3

In Part 3 (about three minutes), you and your partner work together. The examiner will give you both something to look at (map, advertisements, photographs, etc.), and ask you to work together to make a plan, take a decision, solve a problem, etc. While you and your partner are working on the task, the examiner will not say much, but will help you if you have problems. This part of the paper tests your ability to use your English to co-operate with other people on a task. This involves exchanging information and opinions, taking turns and directing the conversation when necessary.

- Make sure you and your partner understand the task before you begin. Don't be afraid to ask the examiner if you are not sure what to do. This can happen just as easily in 'real life', and the ability to deal politely and successfully with difficulties like this can show that you really know how to use your English.

Part 4

In Part 4 (about four minutes), the examiner will ask you both to discuss ideas connected with the work you did in Part 3, and will ask you both questions to give you the chance to cover the topic fully. This part of the paper tests the ability to express opinions and comment appropriately on other people's views. Taking turns and co-operation with your partner can be important here, too.

- The examiner will ask questions to develop ideas from Part 3, but doesn't want to hear you saying the same things over again. Listen carefully to the questions and try to take the discussion into areas which you haven't already discussed.
- In Parts 3 and 4, try to share the time equally with your partner. Ideally, the conversation should pass quite freely between you. If your partner is quiet, you may need to ask direct questions (e.g. *What do you think about…? Do you think that's a good idea?* etc.). If your partner talks a bit too much, you must be prepared to interrupt politely and give your own opinion (e.g. *Yes, I see what you mean, but …*). When you are practising, try to find out whether you are too quiet or talk too much yourself (your friends may help you to decide!). Like any 'real-life' conversation, the exercises work best when the two speakers are aware of each other's needs. There are many good books on spoken English which can help you to learn how to 'manage' a conversation successfully.

Preparing for the examination

- Try to get as much practical speaking experience as you can. You will be with a partner in the Speaking paper, so practise with a partner whenever you can. This may be difficult, or impossible, in your particular situation, but it is difficult to be relaxed about the exercises, or to understand completely how they work, if you haven't had some practice. Ask a friend or relative to help. Even if their English isn't as good as yours, you will get some experience of managing the exercises and the timing – and you'll probably have a good laugh, too.

- You can also play all three parts yourself (examiner and both students). This is not as stupid as it sounds – although you may still want to make sure that no one else can hear you! The main disadvantages are that you don't get any listening practice, and, as you will be in complete control of the situation, you will not have to deal with any unexpected difficulties. If you work like this, don't let your voice go flat. Like a radio announcer, or an actor talking into a telephone on stage, you have to imagine that people are really listening to you.

- Do not spend too long looking at the practice pictures in this book before you actually use them because, in the examination, you will not see the pictures in advance, and will have to think quickly and start talking almost immediately. This is an important skill to practise: you must get used to starting quickly, even if this means you have to start talking before you know exactly what you want to say. You do this all the time in your own language, often by using 'fillers' – phrases which do not mean much in themselves, but give you time to think while you are talking. You can learn to do this in English, too, with phrases like *I'm not sure what the best answer is, but perhaps …*; *I haven't really thought about this before, but I suppose …*, etc. If you have to learn new phrases to do this, make sure you do it early, and get lots of practice with the ones you like. Also, make sure you don't emphasise fillers too strongly. You can probably hear how strange this sounds if you do it in your own language: fillers don't add much to the meaning of what you say, so they don't need strong emphasis.

- **Remember:** the Speaking paper is an opportunity to show your ability, not a threat. The examiners choose the exercises as good starting points for conversation, not to cause you problems on particular points of vocabulary or grammar. However, it is a good idea to make sure that you have enough general vocabulary to be able to talk about any of the 25 topic areas listed on page 28. If nothing else, this will make you feel more confident when you go into the examination room.

- Notice that much of what you have to say in the examination room is **not** directly concerned with the topics of Parts 2, 3 and 4. If you study and practise the language you need in order to introduce yourself, meet new people, express opinions, make suggestions, take turns, disagree politely, apologise for mistakes, etc., you will soon be on the way to a good mark. Skills like these are what the test is really about, not the photographs and diagrams which are used in the various exercises.

- It is also useful to do some work on explaining where something is in a picture or diagram (*the man in the background, the house in the top left-hand corner*) or how it relates to other things in the picture (*the tallest woman, the house opposite the cinema*). Try to avoid pointing things out with your finger.

- Get into the habit of talking about the other work you are doing – texts you have read, films you have seen, articles you have produced for the Writing paper, etc. If you can find someone to listen to you, so much the better, but this is not essential. Too many students learn languages in their heads without getting the words out of their mouths often enough to become really confident. Don't be one of them.

Practice

Practice 1

Part 1

Ask each other about the area where you live. Use questions like these:

> *Where are you from?*
> *What part of ... are you from?*
> *How long have you lived in ... ?*
> *Tell me a bit about the area ...*
> *What's it like living here/there ... ?*
> (If you are not in your home town/country) *What are the main differences between here and your home town/country?*

Each of you should try to talk naturally about these things for about two minutes.

Part 2

One of you looks at pictures 1A and 1B in the Colour Section. Show the pictures to your partner. Talk about your pictures for one minute while your partner listens. Say what your pair of pictures shows. Mention ways in which they are similar and different. Say how you'd feel about studying in similar places. Talk for about one minute. Ask your partner which of them she (or he) would prefer to study in. Now, the person who has been listening talks about pictures 1C and 1D in the same way and then asks the listener which of them she (or he) would prefer to study in.

Part 3

Look at the town plan (1E) together. Consider which of the three locations **A, B** and **C** would be the best site for a new hospital and why. For example, think about the other buildings near each site. Would they be noisy or dirty? Think about transport and traffic. Would the hospital be easy to reach?

Spend about two or three minutes discussing this.

Part 4

Now imagine the examiner joins your conversation and asks you questions. Practise answering questions about what you have been discussing. For example, you can ask each other questions like these:

> *Are cities too noisy?*
> *What can be done to reduce noise pollution in cities?*
> *How important is it that there should be good public transport?*
> *Do people use private cars too much? Why?*
> *Do you think the traffic in cities should be controlled more strictly? How?*
> *Is it important for local people to be involved in planning decisions? Why?*
> *Are local people sufficiently involved in planning decisions on the whole?*
> *If not, why not? What could be done to improve this?*

This part of the test lasts about four minutes.

Practice 2

Part 1

Ask each other about your families. Use questions like these:

Do you have brothers and sisters? Tell me something about them …

Do you get on well together?

What are the advantages/disadvantages of being an only child/member of a large family?

Do you see much of the older members of your family? Your grandparents, for example?

Each of you should try to talk naturally about these things for about two minutes.

Part 2

One of you looks at pictures 2A and 2B in the Colour Section. Show the pictures to your partner. Talk about your pictures for one minute while your partner listens. Say what your pair of pictures shows. Mention ways in which they are similar and different. Say how you'd feel about eating in similar places. Talk for about one minute. Ask your partner which of them she (or he) would prefer to eat in. Now, the person who has been listening talks about pictures 2C and 2D in the same way and then asks the listener which of them she (or he) would prefer to eat in.

Part 3

Look at the gift catalogue (2E) and the pictures of people (2F) together. Discuss which of the presents would be most suitable for each of the people and why. Spend about two or three minutes doing this.

Part 4

Now imagine the examiner joins your conversation and asks you questions. Practise answering questions related to what you have been discussing. For example, you can ask each other questions like these:

Do you enjoy giving people presents? Why/Why not?

How do you decide what to give?

When do people give presents in your country? For example, on birthdays, special occasions … ? What sorts of things do they give?

Are there any traditions in your country about giving or receiving presents? For example, should you open a present immediately when you are given it? Why/Why not?

Do people spend too much money on unnecessary things nowadays, like tourist souvenirs … ?

What sort of things do people buy as souvenirs from your country?

Do you think these are the right sort of things for them to buy?

This part of the test lasts about four minutes.

Practice 3

Part 1

Ask each other about free-time activities. Use questions like these:

> *What do you enjoy doing in your free time?*
> *Tell me a bit about what you actually do when you …*
> *How long have you been interested in … ?*
> *Can you explain something about the rules of / why people enjoy / the attraction of … ?*

Each of you should try to talk naturally about these things for about two minutes.

Part 2

One of you looks at pictures 3A and 3B in the Colour Section. Show the pictures to your partner. Talk about your pictures for one minute while your partner listens. Say what your pair of pictures shows. Mention ways in which they are similar and different. Say how you'd feel about these ways of travelling. Talk for about one minute. Ask your partner which way she (or he) would prefer to travel. Now, the person who has been listening talks about pictures 3C and 3D in the same way and then asks the listener which way she (or he) would prefer to travel.

Part 3

Look at the illustration 'Success in Sport' (3E). Discuss which of the reasons given are most important in deciding whether people are successful in sport and which don't matter so much.

Spend about two or three minutes doing this.

Part 4

Now imagine the examiner joins your conversation and asks you questions.

Practise answering questions related to what you have been discussing. For example, you can ask each other questions like these:

> *Is it better to watch sport on television or live?*
> *Are famous sportspeople good models for young people to follow? Why/Why not?*
> *What dangers are involved in international sport?*
> *Is there too much advertising in sport?*
> *Do people attach too much importance to sports nowadays? Why/Why not?*
> *What could be done to help young sportsmen and women in your area?*
> *Should governments give more support to young sportsmen and women? Why/Why not?*

This part of the test lasts about four minutes.

Practice 4

Part 1

Ask each other about studying English. Use questions like these:

Are you studying English for any special purpose?
In what way do you think English will be useful to you in the future?
If not, why not?
What other languages do you/would you like to study? Why?
Can you tell me about your career plans?
(If you are still at school) *What will you do when you leave school?*

Each of you should try to talk naturally about these things for about two minutes.

Part 2

One of you looks at pictures 4A and 4B in the Colour Section. Show the pictures to your partner. Talk about your pictures for one minute while your partner listens. Say what your pair of pictures shows. Mention ways in which they are similar and different. Say how you'd feel about living in similar places. Talk for about one minute. Ask your partner which of them she (or he) would prefer to live in. Now, the person who has been listening talks about pictures 4C and 4D in the same way and then asks the listener which of them she (or he) would prefer to live in.

Part 3

Look at the photograph (4E). This young woman wants to get a job looking after elderly people. She's going for her interview tomorrow and she needs some advice. Discuss what you should tell her. Should she change her appearance, and if so, how?

Spend about two or three minutes doing this.

Part 4

Now imagine the examiner joins your conversation and asks you questions.

Practise answering questions related to what you have been discussing. For example, you can ask each other questions like these:

Do you think it's important to dress smartly for work?
Have you ever had problems with your teachers or parents about the clothes you wear?
Why do some young people wear very unusual clothes?
Do people's clothes tell you about their personalities?
How much do you care about being in fashion?
Are fashion clothes good value for money?
Do fashions have too much influence on what people buy?

This part of the test lasts about four minutes.

FCE Topics

These are the topics used in the FCE exam:

- Personal life and circumstances e.g. personal experiences
- Living conditions e.g. where/how people live
- Occupations
- Education, study and learning
- Free-time activities
- Travel and tourism
- Consumer goods and shopping
- Eating and drinking
- Social/family relations
- The media
- The weather
- The environment/ecology
- Entertainment
- Health and exercise
- Services e.g. banks, post offices, etc.
- Places
- Language
- Music
- Fashion
- Animals
- Cinema
- History
- The Arts
- Sports
- People

Taking the exam

Some time before the examination takes place, you will be told the dates and times of your papers, and where the examination will be held. Make a careful note of your Centre number and particularly your Candidate number.

Papers 1, 2 and 3 always take place on the same day. Papers 4 and 5 will probably take place on one or two different days close to the written papers. At some centres, all five papers take place on the same day. Whichever is the case at your centre, make sure you understand and follow the instructions carefully and arrive in good time. If the building where the examination is held is new to you, it is a good idea to allow enough time to deal with problems (not being able to find the right entrance, going to the wrong room, etc.), so that you can arrive at your desk calm and ready to start work. This is especially important if you think you may be nervous on the examination day.

Before you start

Check all the examination materials you are given (question papers, answer sheets, marksheet, etc.) to make sure that they are the correct level, i.e. First Certificate, and if they come with a candidate name already printed on, that the material carries your own name. If anything seems to be wrong, tell the supervisor immediately. Do not wait until the end of the examination, when it may be too late to do anything about it.

This is also important in the Listening paper. If you cannot hear the tape properly during the introduction to the examination, you must tell the supervisor immediately. Nothing can be done if you complain after the test.

If for any reason, in any paper, you have to write answers on extra sheets of paper, be sure to write your name, Centre number and Candidate number clearly at the top of each extra sheet. Do this before you begin each sheet: it is too easy to forget at the end. Make sure that any extra sheets are safely attached to the rest of your work.

Writing your answers

For Papers 1, 3 and 4 you will be provided with special answer sheets. You should study the samples at the back of this book carefully and make sure that you understand how to use them. If you can, make photocopies and practise answering on the answer sheets at an early stage, so that you can get used to dealing with them. You do not want to have difficulty with the sheets in the examination itself. In Paper 2, you answer in the question paper booklet (e.g. Test 1 p. 44 and 46).

Many candidates prefer to mark their answers on the question paper first, and then copy them onto the answer sheet later. If you prefer to do this, you must learn to answer the questions quickly enough to allow plenty of time to put your answers on the answer sheet before the end of the paper **without**

rushing. If you have to hurry, you may make mistakes by copying your answers wrongly, or by putting your answers against the wrong question numbers.

Paper 1

1	A B C D E F G H I
2	A B C D E F G H I
3	A B C D E F G H I

For Paper 1 you need a soft pencil and a good quality eraser. Notice that the answer sheet includes nine choices (**A–I**) for each question number, although the question paper itself will have fewer choices for many of the questions (e.g. four choices in Part 2). Just ignore the unnecessary letters. The diagram above shows the answers marked in for Questions 1 and 2 of an imaginary Paper 1. The answer for Question 1 is E and the answer for Question 2 is G. These marks **must** be made in **pencil.** If you change your mind, **you must rub out your first answer completely** since two marks against any question number will automatically be marked wrong. Be sure to work cleanly on the answer sheet. This answer sheet will be 'read' by an electronic 'eye' and any dirty marks may be misinterpreted by it.

Part 4 of Paper 1 may include questions which require more than one answer. For example, a task based on four short texts about different museums might ask:

Which museum:
has recently opened a new building?

22		23	

In this case, you may give the two answers you choose in any order.

This only happens in Part 4 of Paper 1, and you will find that such answers are marked 'interchangeable' in the Key.

- Practise filling in the answer sheet **while you are answering the questions** on Paper 1; don't wait to copy your answers at the end. (Remember, you are allowed to photocopy the answer sheets at the end of this book, so you can have plenty of practice with them.)
- Always make sure you are putting your answer against the correct question number. This is especially important when you leave out a difficult question and move on.
- There are two reasons why it's better to write straight onto the answer sheet. First, you **save time,** which can be important on Paper 1. Second, you **avoid mistakes in** copying.

Paper 2

You must write your answers for Paper 2 in the spaces provided on the question paper. You **must** write in **pen** and you must hand in all your rough notes and plans at the end of the test. If you want to change something, cross it out neatly.

Don't use brackets () for this. Write as clearly as possible. This paper is marked by examiners and tidy, legible work is much appreciated. Bad handwriting or messy changes to your answer can actually lose marks if your final decisions are not clear.

- Remember how important it is to plan your answer before you begin. This should mean that you do not need to change to a new question or rewrite large parts of your answer on the examination paper.

Papers 3 and 4

Paper 3:

Part 1					Part 2	Do not write here
1	A	B	C	D	16	16
2	A	B	C	D	17	17
ͻ	A	B	C	ᴅ	⩒	18

Paper 4:

Part 1				Part 2	Do not write here
1	A	B	C	9	9
2	A	B	C	10	10
ͻ	ᴀ	B	C	⩒⩒	11

For these papers, it is quite a good idea to **write your answers on the question paper** and then **transfer** them to the special answer sheet. There is usually plenty of time during Paper 3 to do this and for Paper 4 you are given five minutes at the end of the test.

Both papers involve two different answering methods.

Paper 3, Part 1 **Paper 4, Parts 1 and 3**	These are like smaller versions of Paper 1. You must answer **in pencil,** and take special care when making any changes (as described for Paper 1 on p. 30).
Paper 3, Parts 2, 3, 4 and 5 **Paper 4, Parts 2 and 4**	In these parts, you must write your answers in the spaces provided. It's best to write **in pen,** although you can use pencil if you wish. Be careful not to make spelling mistakes when you are copying and do not make any marks in the columns headed 'Do not write here'. These are used for marking your answers.

- With the Listening paper, as with the Speaking (see below), it is a good idea to spend the time immediately before your test getting yourself ready to work in English. Find someone to talk to in English, or concentrate quietly on the task ahead. Avoid friends who want to chat in your own language – you will have plenty of time for that afterwards!

Paper 5

It's worth remembering some general advice when you think about the Speaking paper: find out exactly where it is and get there in good time, but not too early if you think this will make you nervous. The supervisor will give you a computerised marksheet to hand to the examiner at the start of your test. This looks similar to the written answer sheets at the back of this book. Make sure it has your name on it – you don't want someone else to get your mark!

You will then go into the exam room with your partner, the examiners will ask you for your marksheet and check that it has the correct name. Then the test begins. Remember that one of the examiners will not be joining in the conversation, and may sit some distance away in a corner. You should concentrate on the examiner working with you (the interlocutor) and on your partner. Do not worry about the other examiner during the test.

At the end of the test, the examiner will thank you both. You should thank the examiners and leave promptly. The examiners will keep your marksheet, and they are not allowed to discuss your marks with you, so do not ask them how you have done.

- You may have a chance to say hello to your exam partner before the test begins. If you do, do not miss this opportunity to get to know each other.
- You will get off to a better start if you have been speaking and/or thinking in English before the examination. This will help you to have your vocabulary close to the front of your mind, and to have your best pronunciation ready. Candidates often make the mistake of spending the last half hour before their test chatting to friends in their own language. Unless you are very good indeed, this is not the best preparation for a test in a foreign language!
- It is also a good idea to go through in your mind what you will have to do in the different parts of the Paper, so that you are ready to do the right job at the right time.
- If you get very nervous, it can be helpful to do some deep-breathing exercises before you go in. Remind yourself that you have done a lot of work for this, and that this is your chance to show it.

Results

When you receive your result, you will be given a **grade** for the whole exam. If you get A (the highest grade), B or C, you have passed, and will receive a **certificate.** If you get D, E or U (Unclassified), you have failed, and will not receive a certificate.

All candidates receive a **results slip.** If you pass the exam, your results slip will mention any papers in which you did particularly well. For example, it might show that your exam grade is C, but you scored particularly good marks in the Speaking paper. If you fail the exam, your results slip will show you the papers in which you did badly. This will help if you decide to try again, because you will know where you need the most practice.

The Practice Tests

Practice Test 1

PAPER 1   READING (1 hour 15 minutes)

PART 1

*You are going to read a newspaper article about children's safety. Choose the most suitable heading from the list (**A–I**) for each part (**1–7**) of the article. There is one extra heading which you do not need to use. There is an example at the beginning (**0**).*

Mark your answers **on the separate answer sheet.**

A	Dangers off the road too
B	Trial period
C	Not what it appears to be
D	Dangerous driving
E	Dangers of fuel
F	First of many?
G	Learning to judge
H	Funds from industry
I	Danger in the city

Crash courses

0	*I*

It is a typical urban scene. Two cars are parked close together at the kerbside and a child is attempting to cross the road from between them. Down the street, another car looms. Houses flank the pavements and around the corner there is a brightly-lit petrol station.

1	

It is all extraordinarily realistic, but it is unreal. For the difference between this and thousands of similar locations throughout the country is that this street is indoors – it is a mock-up designed by studio set-builders from Anglia Television.

2	

We are standing inside a converted warehouse in Milton Keynes, home of a project which is the blueprint for an exciting new way of teaching children safety awareness, especially road safety. It is called Hazard Alley. If the centre proves successful and, having visited it, I am convinced it will, then its imaginative approach could easily be copied throughout the country.

3	

The project was started by the local authority in conjunction with the police. The finance came from commercial sponsorship by companies including Coca-Cola, Volkswagen and Anglia TV. There is already a catchy cartoon character mascot for the centre: Haza, the Hazard Alley cat.

4	

A novel setting for children to be taught and practise a wide range of safety topics, Hazard Alley takes its name from the dark alleyway in the centre of the converted warehouse which links the urban street scene and a series of country sets that focus on rural safety. As well as road drill, children are tutored in home safety and how to avoid trouble in playgrounds, parks, alleyways, near railways and on farmland.

5	

In the street scene, children practise the safe way to cross a road, including coping with parked vehicles, and are given a practical understanding of how long it takes a car to stop when travelling at 30 mph. Could the car they see looming down the road stop in time if a child stepped out between the parked cars? No, it would be through that wall at the end before it finished braking, 23 metres after the driver started to brake.

6	

On the mock-up petrol station forecourt, provided by Shell, the youngsters learn the dangers when filling a vehicle with petrol. They discuss car fires, the flammability of different components, why the car's engine must be switched off and why smoking and using a car phone are illegal on a garage forecourt.

7	

Hazard Alley is gearing up for its official opening, and the local schools which have experienced it so far have been testing out the centre before it launches into a full programme of group visits. It is already proving immensely popular. Eventually it may open to individual family groups. When that happens, it will be well worth a day trip: children will love it and they could learn something which may save their lives.

*You are going to read a magazine article about being liked. For questions **8–15**, choose the answer (**A**, **B**, **C** or **D**) which you think fits best according to the text. Mark your answers **on the separate answer sheet**.*

LOVE ME DO!

I've just got to talk about this problem I'm having with my postman. It all began a year ago, after the birth of his first child. Not wanting to appear rude, I asked him about the baby. The next week, not wanting him to think I had asked out of mere politeness the week before, I asked all about the baby again. Now I can't break the habit. I freeze whenever I see him coming. The words 'How's the baby?' come out on their own. It's annoying. It holds me up. It holds him up. So why can't I stop it?

The answer, of course, is that I want him to like me. Come to think of it, I want everyone to like me. This was made clear to me the other day. I found myself in the bank, replying 'Oh, as it comes' when the cashier asked how I'd like the money. Even as she was handing me the £20 note, I realised I'd have no small change with which to buy my newspaper. But, not wanting her to dislike me (she'd already written '1 x £20' on the back of my cheque), said nothing.

In order to get the £20 note down to a decent, paper-buying size, I went into the grocer's. Not wanting to buy things I didn't actually need (I do have some pride, you know), I bought some large cans of beans and a frozen chicken for dinner that night. That got the price up to a respectable £5.12, which I duly paid. I then bought my paper at the station with my hard-gained £5 note.

With my sister, it wasn't the postman who was the problem, but the caretaker of her block of flats: 'All he ever does is moan and complain; he talks at me rather than to me, never listens to a word I say, and yet for some reason I'm always really nice to him. I'm worried in case I have a domestic crisis one day, and he won't lift a finger to help.'

I have a friend called Stephen, who is a prisoner of the call-waiting device he has had installed on his phone. 'I get this beeping sound to tell me there's another call on the line, but I can never bring myself to interrupt the person I'm talking to. So I end up not concentrating on what the first person's saying, while at the same time annoying the person who's trying to get through.'

What about at work? Richard Lawton, a management trainer, warns: 'Those managers who are actually liked by most of their staff are always those to whom being liked is not the primary goal. The qualities that make managers popular are being honest with staff, treating them as human beings and observing common courtesies like saying hello in the morning.' To illustrate the point, Richard cites the story of the company chairman who desperately wanted to be liked and who, after making one of his managers redundant, said with moist eyes that he was so, so sorry the man was leaving. To which the embittered employee replied: 'If you were that sorry, I wouldn't be leaving.' The lesson being, therefore, that if you try too hard to be liked, people won't like you.

The experts say it all starts in childhood. 'If children feel they can only get love from their parents by being good,' says Zelda West-Meads, a marriage guidance consultant, 'they develop low self-confidence and become compulsive givers.' But is there anything wrong in being a giver, the world not being exactly short of takers? Anne Cousins believes there is. 'There is a point at which giving becomes unhealthy,' she says. 'It comes when you do things for others but feel bad about it.'

I am now trying hard to say to people 'I feel uncomfortable about saying this, but ...', and tell myself 'Refusal of a request does not mean rejection of a person' and I find I can say almost anything to almost anyone.

8 Why does the writer ask the postman about his baby?
A He is interested in the baby.
B He wants to create a good impression.
C The postman is always polite to him.
D The postman enjoys a chat.

9 The writer went into the grocer's so that
A he had some food for dinner that night.
B he could buy a newspaper there.
C he could ask for £20 in change.
D he could buy something to get some change.

10 What do we find out about the writer's sister and the caretaker?
A She doesn't want to risk offending him.
B She doesn't pay attention to him.
C He refuses to help her.
D He asks her for advice.

11 How does Stephen feel about his call-waiting equipment?
A He gets annoyed when it interrupts him.
B He is unable to use it effectively.
C He finds it a relief from long conversations.
D He doesn't think it works properly.

12 Managers are more likely to be popular if they
A help staff with their problems.
B make sure the staff do not lose their jobs.
C encourage staff to be polite to each other.
D do not make too much effort to be liked.

13 When is it wrong to be 'a giver'?
A when it makes you ill
B when it does not give you pleasure
C when you make other people unhappy
D when you are unable to take from others

14 What do we learn from this article?
A If you tell the truth, it will not make people like you less.
B If you take time to talk to people, they will like you better.
C You should avoid unpleasant situations where possible.
D You shouldn't refuse other people's requests for help.

15 Why was this article written?
A to analyse the kinds of conversations people have
B to persuade people to be more polite to each other
C to encourage people to have more self-confidence
D to suggest ways of dealing with difficult people

PART 3

*You are going to read a magazine article about a woman who goes gliding. Seven paragraphs have been removed from the article. Choose from the paragraphs (**A–H**) the one which fits each gap (**16–21**). There is one extra paragraph which you do not need to use. There is an example at the beginning (**0**).*
*Mark your answers **on the separate answer sheet**.*

IN PERSON

Twelve months ago, it was Lyn Ferguson who had the honour of cutting the ribbon to declare our Oakham Distribution Centre and offices open.

| 0 | *H* |

'I had my first glider flight when I was sixteen, but it wasn't until January 1986 that I took it up seriously. My boys had gone to school, I had lots of spare time and I thought, 'What am I going to do?' It just so happened that I had the opportunity to go up in a glider as a passenger to see if I liked it. I did.'

| 16 | |

'Really, it's very easy. All you need is coordination. The average person needs about 60 flights before they can go solo, completely alone, which sounds a lot, but the average instruction flight only takes around eight minutes, so training doesn't take long. I once did eleven trips in a day when I was training.'

| 17 | |

'Well, once you've done it alone, you can register with the British Gliding Association, then work towards your Bronze Badge. Each badge after that is about height, distance and endurance.

| 18 | |

Then, there are 10 km flights (straight out and back to the beginning), and 300 km flights, which show navigation skills. They're flown in a triangle starting and finishing at the airfield.'

| 19 | |

'Once, when I was in Australia, I lost height whilst attempting a 300 km flight and had to select a field to land in. Luckily, I spotted a field with a tractor in it and was able to land there. I think the farmer was pretty surprised when a glider suddenly landed next to him! He did let me use his phone, though.'

| 20 | |

'When you have a student who's finding things difficult, you convince them that they can do it. When they do, they're so pleased with themselves. When you land and they say "I can do it", it's brilliant.'

| 21 | |

'Flying is the main part, but there are other angles too. Gliding is like everything else. What you put in is what you get out. It's all about team work too. Everybody mucks in to push gliders around, pull cables in and generally help out. You can't do it on your own. I've met people in gliding from all walks of life, from lots of different countries, that I would never have met if I didn't go gliding.'

So, next time you see a glider soaring overhead, it may well be Lyn flying her way to another badge or, knowing her love of the sport, just gliding for the sheer fun of it.

A After eight years' gliding experience, Lyn has achieved her Bronze and Silver Badges and is an Assistant Rated Instructor. She hopes to go on and earn more badges, as well as becoming a Full Rated Instructor in the future. Her role as an instructor provides her with some of gliding's most rewarding moments.

B To those of us on the ground gazing up, the pilot's skills are there for all to see, as the glider soars effortlessly on the warm air thermals. Lyn is not one to boast about her training though.

C But for all the achievement of solo flight, glider pilots have to work for one another, and this is another side of gliding that Lyn enjoys and appreciates.

D So with the first solo flight behind you, what's next?

E Lyn thinks for a moment when she's asked if she's ever had any emergencies to contend with.

F As a result, a friend of hers flew in a glider alongside her along the Innsbruck Valley at mountain top height ... that's around seven thousand, four hundred feet.

G To get the Silver, for example, you have to get over 1,000 m in height, complete a five-hour flight and then a 50 km flight to a designated airfield.

H As PA to our Managing Director, Lyn has to be pretty level-headed, but in her spare time, she likes nothing better than to have her head in the clouds, indulging in her passion for gliding.

PART 4

You are going to read some information about airports in Britain. For questions **22–35**, choose from the airports (**A–H**). Some of the airports may be chosen more than once. When more than one answer is required, these may be given in any order. There is an example at the beginning (**0**).
Mark your answers **on the separate answer sheet**.

Which airport:

does not sell anything to read?	**0**	*H*		
has shops which sell highly-priced goods?	**22**		**23**	
seems to have put its seating in the wrong place?	**24**			
makes it very easy for passengers to find their way through?	**25**			
has its shops spread out?	**26**			
has a departure lounge which is not very impressive?	**27**		**28**	
has a badly-situated café?	**29**			
changes its range of food according to the season?	**30**			
has an unexpectedly disappointing range of shops?	**31**			
has a good view of the planes?	**32**			
has facilities for people who are travelling for work?	**33**		**34**	
needs modernising?	**35**			

Which airport?

The choice of where to fly from has never been greater, particularly for those flying on a package holiday. For each airport, we looked at the facilities (e.g. restaurants, waiting areas, etc.) offered before going through passport control (land-side) and after going through passport control (air-side).

A   Heathrow 4

The check-in hall is spacious and modern. There are few land-side shops but the essentials are available. A café with pine seating and a medium range of hot dishes and salads is situated upstairs. There are more facilities air-side. The shops are clustered into the central part of the 500-metre long hall, and expensive ranges are well represented. There's plenty of natural light from the windows that overlook the runway and lots of seating away from the shopping area.

B   Manchester 2

The check-in hall has a high glass roof which lets in natural light. The café is at one end and slightly separated from the rest of the facilities, which makes it much more pleasant. There's also an up-market coffee shop. Hundreds of seats – little used when we visited despite the passengers crowded below – are available upstairs. The departure lounge is bright and has plenty of space, the cafeteria is pleasant.

C   Stansted

Passengers can walk in a straight line from the entrance, through the check-in to the monorail that takes them to their plane. Land-side, ⟫→

41

there's a cluster of fast food outlets that sell baked potatoes, American burgers and filled rolls. All seating is in the same area away from the check-in and shops. There's a surprisingly small number of shops considering Stansted's claims to be a major London airport, although basic stores like a chemist and bookshop are here. The large departure lounge has blue seats and grey carpet. There's a large tax-free and luxury goods shopping area and a café.

D Heathrow 2

Avoid travelling from here if you can. The check-in area is unpleasant with a claustrophobic low roof and scores of pillars. The upstairs café is noisy because it is next to the music shop. The departure lounge is also too small with illuminated advertisements hanging from its low ceiling.

E Manchester 1

The large, low check-in hall is the least impressive part of the terminal. Beyond that is a pleasant shopping mall with a wide range of shops and snack bars. The self-service eating area has a good range of foods from steak and chips to salads. There is also a more formal restaurant mostly used for business lunches. The departure lounge is large and bright.

F Edinburgh

The eating options range from a coffee shop to a self-service restaurant, and a reasonable variety of shops are scattered around the land-side area rather than being collected in one area. The air-side food arrangements are mainly limited to rolls and buns.

G East Midlands

The check-in area is in a long, low building where the roof is supported by a forest of pillars which interrupt the line of vision. There's a café and bar upstairs along with a pizza restaurant during the summer. The main eating area is downstairs and mainly serves sandwiches and cakes along with a hot dish of the day. The departure lounge is pleasant with natural light and plenty of dark blue seats. The Sherwood Lounge has easy chairs and sofas and is aimed at commercial travellers.

H Cardiff

The facilities are simple and the decoration is showing its age. Shopping is extremely limited with only bare essentials available. There are no books or magazines for sale. The restaurant is unappealing. The tiny departure lounge is dark and uninviting.

PAPER 2   WRITING (1 hour 30 minutes)

PART 1

*You **must** answer this question.*

1   You are interested in attending a language course in England next summer. You have seen the advertisement below. You have also talked to your English teacher and she has suggested some things that you should check before you register.

Read the advertisement below, together with your teacher's note. Then write to the language school, asking for information about the points mentioned by your teacher, and anything else that you think is important.

SUMMER LANGUAGE COURSES

2 weeks, 3 weeks, 1 month

Beautiful English market town. Full sports and social programme. Accommodation with friendly English families. Helpful teachers. Small classes.

Full details from: Ian Lawrence, The Smart School of English, High Street, Little Bonnington

It's a great idea for you to do a language course in England. Be careful to choose a good school. When you write, ask about these things:
- student numbers, ages
- details of sports programme etc.
- local facilities
- teachers' qualifications
Let me know if you need any more help. Good luck!

Write **a letter** of between **120–180** words in an appropriate style on the next page. Do not write any addresses.

PART 1

....

....

....

....

....

....

....

....

....

....

....

....

....

....

....

....

....

....

....

....

....

....

....

....

....

....

....

....

....

PART 2

*Write an answer to **one** of the questions **2–5** in this part. Write your answer in*
***120–180** words in an appropriate style on the next page, putting the question*
number in the box.

2   An international young people's magazine is investigating the question:
    Do young people today really know what they want from life?

    Write a short **article** for this magazine on this topic based on your own
    experience.

3   You have decided to enter this competition.

Exciting chance for writers!

Write a short story and win a Great Prize

Your entry must begin or end with the
following words:

*No matter what people said about
Alex, I knew he was a true friend.*

Write your **story** for the competition.

4   You are attending a summer language course and have been asked to report
    on a local leisure facility (e.g. cinema, sports hall, etc) for the benefit of
    students attending the next course.

    Write your **report** describing the facility and what it has to offer, and
    commenting on its good and bad points.

5   **Background reading texts**

    Answer **one** of the following two questions based on your reading of **one** of
    the set books (see p.2). Write the title of the book next to the question number
    box.

    Either **(a)** Describe your favourite character in the book and explain what
                you like about him/her.

    or   **(b)** Explain how the physical setting of the book is important to the
                success of the story.

PART 2

Question	

....

....

....

....

....

....

....

....

....

....

....

....

....

....

....

....

....

....

....

....

....

....

....

....

....

PAPER 3   USE OF ENGLISH (1 hour 15 minutes)

PART 1

For questions **1–15**, *read the text below and decide which answer* **A, B, C** *or* **D**
best fits each space. There is an example at the beginning (**0**).
Mark your answers **on the separate answer sheet.**

Example:

0   **A** expect   **B** count   **C** claim   **D** prepare

0	A	B	C	D
	▬	▬	▬	▬

ACTION SCENES IN FILMS

Modern cinema audiences **(0)** .... to see plenty of thrilling scenes in action films.
These scenes, which are **(1)** .... as stunts, are usually **(2)** .... by stuntmen who are
specially trained to do dangerous things safely. **(3)** .... can crash a car, but if you're
shooting a film, you have to be extremely **(4)** .... , sometimes stopping **(5)** .... in front
of the camera and film crew. At an early **(6)** .... in the production, an expert
stuntman is **(7)** .... in to work out the action scenes and form a team. He is the only
person who can go **(8)** .... the wishes of the director, **(9)** .... he will usually only do
this in the **(10)** .... of safety.

Many famous actors like to do the dangerous parts themselves, which produces
better shots, since stuntmen don't have to **(11)** .... in for the actors. Actors like to
become **(12)** .... in all the important aspects of the character they are playing, but
without the recent progress in safety equipment, insurance companies would
never **(13)** .... them take the risk. To do their own stunts, actors need to be good
athletes, but they must also be sensible and know their **(14)** .... . If they were to be
hurt, the film would **(15)** .... to a sudden halt.

1   **A** remarked   **B** known   **C** referred   **D** named

2   **A** performed   **B** given   **C** fulfilled   **D** displayed

3   **A** Everyone   **B** Someone   **C** Anyone   **D** No-one

4   **A** detailed   **B** plain   **C** straight   **D** precise

5   **A** right   **B** exact   **C** direct   **D** strict

6   **A** period   **B** minute   **C** part   **D** stage

7   **A** led   **B** taken   **C** drawn   **D** called

8   **A** over   **B** against   **C** through   **D** across

9   **A** despite   **B** so   **C** although   **D** otherwise

10 **A** interests   **B** needs   **C** purposes   **D** regards

11 **A** work   **B** get   **C** put   **D** stand

12 **A** connected   **B** arranged   **C** involved   **D** affected

13 **A** allow   **B** let   **C** permit   **D** admit

14 **A** limits   **B** ends   **C** frontiers   **D** borders

15 **A** come   **B** fall   **C** pull   **D** go

PART 2

*For questions **16–30**, read the text below and think of the word which best fits each space. Use only **one** word in each space. There is an example at the beginning (**0**).*
*Write your word **on the separate answer sheet**.*

Example:

0	*or*	0

SHARKS

For anyone who wants either to film **(0)** .... study great white sharks, Australian expert, Rodney Fox, is the first contact. Fox knows exactly **(16)** .... the sharks will be at different times of the year; and can even predict **(17)** .... they will behave around blood, divers and other sharks. He understands them as well as **(18)** .... else alive. In fact, he's lucky to *be* alive; a 'great white' once **(19)** .... to bite him in half.

Three decades **(20)** .... this near-fatal attack, Fox still carries the physical scars, but feels **(21)** .... hate for his attacker. Instead he organises three or four trips **(22)** .... year to bring scientists and photographers to the kingdom of the great white shark. **(23)** .... main aim of these trips is to improve people's understanding of an animal **(24)** .... evil reputation has become an excuse for killing it.

Great white sharks are not as amusing as dolphins and seals, **(25)** .... their role in the ocean is critical. They kill off sick animals, helping to prevent the spread **(26)** .... disease and to maintain the balance in the ocean's food chains. Fox feels a responsibility to act **(27)** .... a guardian of great white sharks. **(28)** .... the scientists, film makers and photographers can communicate their sense of wonder **(29)** .... other people, he is confident that understanding **(30)** .... replace hatred.

PART 3

*For questions **31–40**, complete the second sentence so that it has a similar meaning to the first sentence, using the word given. **Do not change the word given**. You must use between two and five words, including the word given. There is an example at the beginning (**0**).*
*Write **only** the missing words **on the separate answer sheet**.*

Example:

0   I last saw him at my 21st birthday party.
    since

    I .... my 21st birthday party.

The gap can be filled by the words 'haven't seen him since' so you write:

0	*haven't seen him since*	0	0 1 2

31   'You've broken my radio, Frank!' said Jane.
    accused

    Jane .... her radio.

32   My car really needs to be repaired soon.
    must

    I really .... repaired soon.

33   Susan regrets not buying that house.
    wishes

    Susan .... that house.

34   I could never have succeeded without your help.
    you

    I could never have succeeded .... me.

35   I thought I might run out of cash, so I took my cheque-book with me.
    case

    I took my cheque-book with me .... out of cash.

36 Linda's plans for a picnic have been spoilt by the weather.
fallen

Linda's plans for a picnic .... because of the weather.

37 The bread was too stale to eat.
fresh

The bread .... to eat.

38 Perhaps Brian went home early.
may

Brian .... home early.

39 I can't possibly work in all this noise!
impossible

It .... work in all this noise!

40 The thief suddenly realised that the police were watching him.
watched

The thief suddenly realised that he .... by the police.

PART 4

*For questions **41–55**, read the text below and look carefully at each line. Some of the lines are correct, and some have a word which should not be there. If a line is correct, put a tick (✓) by the number **on the separate answer sheet**. If a line has a word which should **not** be there, write the word **on the separate answer sheet**. There are two examples at the beginning (**0** and **00**).*

0	✓	0

Examples:

00	*own*	0

WHY I DISLIKE COMPUTERS

0	Almost everyone says that computers are wonderful and that they are
00	changing our own lives for the better by making everything faster and
41	more reliable, but I'm not so much sure that this is the case.
42	The other day I was standing in a large department store until
43	waiting to pay for a couple of films for my camera when the assistant
44	announced that the computer which controlled the till it had stopped
45	working. I didn't think this was a big problem and I set myself off to
46	find another counter, but of course, all the machines are one part of
47	the same system. So there we were: a shop full of customers, money
48	at the ready, waiting to make our purchases, but it was quite clear that
49	none out of the assistants knew what to do. They weren't allowed to
50	take our money and give to customers a written receipt, because the
51	sales wouldn't then have been recorded on the computer system.
52	In the end, like with many other people, I left my shopping on the
53	counter and walked out. Don't you think so that's ridiculous? It would
54	never have happened before computers, and that, for me, is all the
55	problem: we are beginning to depend on these machines for so
	completely that we simply can't manage without them any more.

PART 5

*For questions **56–65**, read the text below. Use the word given in capitals at the end of each line to form a word that fits in the space in the same line. There is an example at the beginning **(0)**. Write your word **on the separate answer sheet**.*

Example:

0	*unusual*	0

CAMERON PARK

At first light, there is nothing **(0)** .... about the town of Cameron Park   **USUAL**
in California but, as the day begins and the town comes to **(56)** .... ,   **LIVE**
you can't help **(57)** .... that, among the cars, there are light aeroplanes   **NOTICE**
moving along the roads towards the airport.

When the town was **(58)** .... built, a small airport was included for the   **ORIGIN**
(59) .... of people flying in to look at the properties which were for   **CONVENIENT**
(60) .... , but it soon became clear to the developers that this was an   **SELL**
attraction in itself. The streets were **(61)** .... so that planes could use   **WIDE**
them, the mailboxes near the road were made **(62)** .... to avoid   **SHORT**
passing wings, and all the electricity cables were buried **(63)** .... .   **GROUND**

Now, there is every **(64)** .... that the residents will have a private   **LIKELY**
plane in their garage and use it with the same **(65)** .... other people   **FREE**
enjoy with their cars.

PAPER 4   LISTENING (approximately 40 minutes)

PART 1

You will hear people talking in eight different situations.
*For questions **1–8**, choose the best answer **A, B** or **C**.*

1   You are visiting a museum when you hear this man addressing a group of
people.
Who is he?

   A   a security guard

   B   a tourist guide

   C   a museum guide

	1

2   You're in a restaurant when you overhear one of the waiters talking.
Who is he talking about?

   A   a colleague

   B   the manager

   C   a customer

	2

3   You're waiting in a hospital corridor when you hear this woman talking.
What does she say about her doctor?

   A   He's made a mistake.

   B   He's been unhelpful.

   C   He's been untruthful.

	3

4   You are out shopping when you hear a shop assistant talking to a customer.
What is she refusing to do?

   A   give him some money

   B   change a faulty item

   C   repair something

	4

5 Listen to this woman introducing the next speaker at a conference.
Why has she been asked to introduce him?

   A He is an old friend.

   B He is a former student of hers.

   C He is a colleague.

> 5

6 You are staying in a farmhouse when you hear your host on the telephone.
Who is he talking to?

   A a supplier

   B a customer

   C an employee

> 6

7 You hear this critic talking on the radio.
What is she recommending?

   A a film

   B a book

   C an exhibition

> 7

8 You are walking up the street when you hear this man talking to a woman at
her front door.
What does he want to do?

   A interview her

   B help her

   C advise her

> 8

PART 2

You will hear a student called Bill talking about his holiday job.
*For questions **9–18**, complete the notes which summarise what he says. You will*
need to write a word or a short phrase in the box.

Reason for doing job:	**9**
Building used to be a	**10**
Good position because it's near	**11**
Main alteration: owner has added	**12**
Bill's favourite task:	**13**
Owner is very careful about	**14**
Attitude of male residents to staff:	**15**
Problem with woman who thought he was	**16**
Other staff treated Bill as	**17**
Bill is going back in order to	**18**

PART 3

You will hear five different women talking about parties.
*For questions **19–23**, choose from the list **A–F** what they describe. Use the letters only once. There is one extra letter which you do not need to use.*

A   She regretted having gone.

B   She was surprised she enjoyed it.

C   She was embarrassed by her friends.

D   She thought it was badly organised.

E   She hadn't known what sort of event it was.

F   She met someone who admired her.

Speaker 1		19
Speaker 2		20
Speaker 3		21
Speaker 4		22
Speaker 5		23

PART 4

You will hear a conversation between two teenagers, Nick and Sandra.
*For questions **24–30**, decide which statements are true or false and mark your*
*answers **T** for True or **F** for False.*

24   Sandra had to do some housework before coming out. | | 24 |

25   Sandra envies Nick. | | 25 |

26   Sandra is angry with her mother. | | 26 |

27   Sandra has failed her exams. | | 27 |

28   Nick sympathises with Sandra's mother. | | 28 |

29   Sandra has lost the tickets. | | 29 |

30   Nick will go to the next concert on his own. | | 30 |

PAPER 5   SPEAKING (approximately 15 minutes)

Part 1

You tell the examiner about yourself. The examiner may ask you questions such as: Where are you from? How do you usually spend your free time? What are your plans for the future? Your partner does the same.

Part 2

The examiner gives you two pictures to look at and asks you to talk about them for about a minute. Your partner does the same with two different pictures.

Part 3

The examiner gives you a photograph or drawing to look at with your partner. You are asked to solve a problem or come to a decision about something in the picture. For example, you might be asked to decide the best way to use some rooms in a language school. You discuss the problem together.

Part 4

You are asked more questions connected with your discussion in Part 3. For example, you might be asked to talk about the best ways of studying.

Practice Test 2

PART 1

You are going to read a magazine article about exercising in water. Choose from the list (A–I) the sentence which best summarises each part (1–7) of the article. There is one extra sentence which you do not need to use. There is an example at the beginning (0).
Mark your answers on the separate answer sheet.

A	You are unlikely to cause yourself an injury in water.
B	It is not as easy as it looks.
C	Aqua fitness can do more than simply help heal injuries.
D	You can lose weight and enjoy yourself at the same time.
E	You can strengthen your heart and muscles by training every day.
F	Your body will adapt to exercising in water.
G	Don't worry about what you look like.
H	Exercise in water puts less pressure on the heart.
I	The idea of exercising in water is not new.

Making a SPLASH

0	*I*

The last thing many people expect to do in a swimming pool these days is swim. The latest fitness phenomenon to make a big splash at the local pool is aqua fitness. The properties of water have long been known to make it one of the safest and most effective media in which to exercise. Physiotherapists have used it for years and, even as far back as the Romans, the value of water for healing has been recognised.

1	

Today 'aqua fitness', as it is known, has seen exercising in the swimming pool progressing from merely being an activity for the recovery of an injury. Aqua fitness has become a valuable training aid even for professional athletes who use it to reduce the risk of overtraining. However, that's not to say that exercising in water isn't ideal for the rest of us too, from the young to the old, from the fit to those who do suffer from complaints such as arthritis.

2	

Exercising in water raises the heart rate less than land aerobics. Lydia Campbell, a fitness expert, says there are no conclusive studies on why it has a less drastic effect on your heart, but there are some factors that partly explain it. Lydia says, 'Water is supportive, as we all know, and with blood flowing more easily, there is less stress on the heart.'

3	

There are other benefits to working out in water such as the fact that your muscles are less likely to ache the following day, the water has a massaging effect on the body, and of course, there is always the possibility of getting a bit slimmer. It is generally thought that an aqua fitness workout can use from 450 to 700 calories an hour. And don't forget, water is fun – exercising to music in water is a unique experience!

4	

The reassuring element of exercising in water is that, apart from doing you good, it is relatively difficult to do anything that is going to harm you.

5	

As far as modesty is concerned, if you miss a step, carry a little more excess weight than you feel comfortable with or just feel embarrassed because you haven't exercised before, there is no need to be anxious as everything is hidden beneath the water level!

6	

Getting used to moving in water takes a little time because of the gravity changes on the body. Running in water will be easier if your body has lots of muscle, but don't worry about this not being the case, as the exercising in water will strengthen muscles anyway. Soon you will be able to move more strongly through the pool.

7	

Classes usually start with a warm-up aimed at stimulating and raising the body temperature. Using the properties of water in an aqua workout can create an effective training programme that might change some previous ideas about how easy exercising in water is. Try running in shallow knee-deep water. It's easy, but try running in thigh-deep water and things suddenly get more difficult – chest-deep water is even harder, as the water resistance increases.

PART 2

You are going to read a newspaper article about a television presenter called Sue Barker. For questions 8–15, choose the answer (A, B, C or D) which you think fits best according to the text.
Mark your answers on the separate answer sheet.

SUE BARKER, the former tennis star, is to present the BBC TV Sports Programme *Grandstand* this summer. The BBC will shortly announce her promotion to one of television's top sports posts, confirming a rise in the media ranks that has been almost as rapid as her progress up the ladder of international tennis in the 1970s.

It is a remarkable comeback to national fame for a woman originally known for being the girlfriend of a pop star and for being a British player who won the French Open tennis tournament.

Her new media career is already very successful. It had a sudden beginning. A succession of injuries and a fall in her ranking from 16th to 63rd caused her to announce her retirement from the game in a dramatic on-court speech at the Australian Open tournament in 1984.

'I took the car back to my hotel where a message was waiting for me to ring a TV station in Sydney. I thought, "Oh God, not another interview", but they asked me to come and start on their sports programme the next day to give expert comment. There was no training, nothing.'

There was no training either when David Hill, then head of sport on Sky TV, recruited her two years ago to be one of the presenters on its Saturday sports programme.

'I turned up and was told my first broadcast was in a few minutes' time. It was a classic, absolutely awful. I rattled through it, it wasn't even making sense, and then I was left for the last four seconds just smiling at the camera.

'It was the longest four seconds of my life. Afterwards I said I wanted to give up, but David said, "You've only made two mistakes, I never sack anyone until they've made three". So I carried on doing five-minute slots – the sports news round-ups – which proved to be very good on-the-job training. Then came the approach from the BBC.'

While Sky took a quiet pride in the fact that the BBC wanted to sign up its star, its annoyance at losing Barker was understandable. It had allowed the BBC to have her for the tennis season and offered a half-and-half arrangement when the BBC wanted to sign her full-time – but the BBC was not interested. Sam Chisholm, Sky's chief executive, decided to take legal action.

In the BBC's tennis team, the strengths of Sue Barker were immediately obvious. She offered a number of technical insights, not just into the game but into the players' mental state, and was not afraid to be critical of those on the court who are still friends, a rare quality among the large number of former sports stars that fill the BBC commentary boxes.

For Barker, being a critic was not always easy, especially as she mixed socially with the players. They did sometimes get upset about it. 'Martina Navratilova watches everything, absolutely everything, and she came up to me quite angry one day, saying "I heard you, I heard what you said about Steffi Graf". But I will tell them exactly why I thought they weren't playing well, compare their performance with a previous one and, if they can honestly say to me they did play well, then I will apologise.'

Having been angry at some of the criticism of *her* during her 13 years of playing international tennis, she feels she can turn that knowledge to good use. 'I know what hurts and what doesn't hurt, and athletes tend to trust other athletes.'

8   What does the writer say about Sue Barker's career?
    A   She took a long time to become famous as a tennis star.
    B   She is better known as a TV presenter than a tennis star.
    C   She obtained an important TV job after a short time.
    D   She has tried a career in pop music.

9   What does 'it' in line 10 refer to?
    A   her tennis career
    B   her comeback
    C   her success on TV
    D   her fame

10 She became a sports commentator because
    A   she was advised to do so by tennis experts.
    B   an Australian TV channel suggested it.
    C   she decided she would prefer it to tennis.
    D   she was tired of being interviewed by other people.

11 What happened when she presented a Saturday sports programme?
    A   She made a better impression than she expected.
    B   The TV company liked the way she smiled at the camera.
    C   She talked for too long and too fast.
    D   The boss wasn't sure whether to sack her or not.

12 How did Sky TV feel when the BBC employed her?
    A   They turned down the offer to share her.
    B   They were glad for her sake.
    C   They did not want to lose her.
    D   They had expected this to happen.

13 How is she different from other sports commentators?
    A   She still has a lot of friends in the game.
    B   She has very good technical background.
    C   She finds it difficult to praise the players.
    D   She speaks the truth about friends.

14 What does she feel she can offer as a sports commentator?
    A   She can give athletes advice on dealing with the camera.
    B   She can make comments which athletes accept.
    C   She can help athletes to get on with each other.
    D   She can attract new viewers to sports programmes.

15 This article was written about Sue Barker because
    A   she is going to be in the public view a lot.
    B   there is a court case between Sky TV and the BBC.
    C   she has recently given up tennis.
    D   a well-known tennis star was recently upset by her.

*You are going to read a newspaper article about an artist. Seven paragraphs have been removed from the article. Choose from the paragraphs (**A–H**) the one which fits each gap (**16–21**). There is one extra paragraph which you do not need to use. There is an example at the beginning (**0**).*

*Mark your answers **on the separate answer sheet**.*

The life of Georgia O'Keeffe

Georgia O'Keeffe was born in 1887 and grew up in Sun Prairie, Wisconsin, a farming town settled only 40 years earlier.

0	*H*

When she was 16, her family moved to Virginia, and O'Keeffe studied art at the Art Institute of Chicago. At 23, she had a crisis of confidence and spoke of giving up painting, but over the next two years she taught art in Texas and in South Carolina, and eventually regained her desire to paint.

16	

O'Keeffe lived and studied in New York on and off for three years, taking time off to teach in Virginia, South Carolina and again in Texas. Always independent-minded, in Texas she became known for her strange clothes.

17	

A friend showed O'Keeffe's drawings to Alfred Stieglitz, the greatest photographer in America and owner of the forward-looking 291 Gallery in New York. When he unwrapped O'Keeffe's charcoal drawings,

he was amazed. 'I realised that I had never seen anything like it before.'

18	

A year later, O'Keeffe gave up her teaching and started painting full-time in Manhattan, Maine and at the Stieglitz family home in Lake George, New York. She also joined Stieglitz's circle of friends, which included some of the most important writers, painters and photographers in America.

19	

While her work grew in confidence, her life with Stieglitz was full of difficulties. He encouraged her work but wanted her to be an obedient wife. In his role as her dealer he sought dictatorial control over the sale and exhibition of her work. O'Keeffe felt imprisoned by her marriage, genuinely loving though it was.

20	

And it gave rise to some of her greatest paintings: landscapes, studies of architecture, and still-lifes. In still-life she became obsessed with the animal skeletons she had collected in the desert.

21	

When Georgia O'Keeffe died, she was a year short of her century. Relatives gave some of O'Keeffe's work to American museums. They show the courage and persistence of one of the most remarkable of all women painters.

A During this period, O'Keeffe made a series of charcoal studies which she called her 'Special' drawings. These were the first work of her artistic maturity. And they were to lead to her first great romantic involvement.

B After Stieglitz died, O'Keeffe rarely visited the East Coast, and the life she led in New Mexico was increasingly solitary. She continued to work, though with decreasing energy (she was now 60 years old). Her work grew steadily in value and she became a very rich woman.

C Stieglitz exhibited the drawings without O'Keeffe's knowledge. Though initially outraged, she knew that 291 was the best possible venue for her work – and Stieglitz himself the best possible dealer. With time, he became equally passionate about O'Keeffe herself. She was 30 and Stieglitz was 53. In 1924 they married.

D She found her escape in New Mexico. She had long preferred the empty landscapes of the American West to the greenery of the East Coast. Even though she remained devoted to the ageing Stieglitz and spent winters with him in New York, New Mexico was her home for the rest of her life.

E The role did not entirely suit her. Solitary by nature and the only woman artist in a group of opinionated men, she was very aware of the oppression of women. Some of the men resented her, feeling threatened by a woman of such exceptional talent.

F O'Keeffe denied the connection and late in life she abruptly finished an interview when asked about it. She also painted New York's cityscape as well as rural architecture.

G O'Keeffe did not feel that her future lay in teaching, but then as now there were few other ways for an artist to earn a living. So she decided to take a teaching degree in New York, and her life was changed forever.

H O'Keeffe was drawn towards art from an early age. She was brilliant at drawing and, at 13, told a friend, 'I'm going to be an artist'.

PART 4

You are going to read a magazine article about New York cafés. For questions
22–34, *choose from the cafés* (**A–H**). *Some of the cafés may be chosen more than once. When more than one answer is required, these may be given in any order. There is an example at the beginning* (**0**).
For question **35**, *choose the answer* (**A**, **B**, **C** *or* **D**) *which you think fits best according to the text.*
Mark your answers **on the separate answer sheet**.

Which of the cafés:

is close to a theatre?	**0**	*H*
does not have very interesting food?	**22**	
is near a well-known monument?	**23**	
is floating?	**24**	
offers some dishes for the health-conscious?	**25**	
is good for sitting and watching others?	**26**	**27**
appeals particularly to tourists?	**28**	
may offer you the chance of some physical exercise?	**29**	
is known by few people?	**30**	
is fairly cheap?	**31**	
has exciting American food?	**32**	
is good for a special evening out?	**33**	**34**

35 The purpose of the text is to
  A identify the liveliest outdoor café in New York.
  B identify the outdoor café in New York with the best food.
  C offer information about a range of eating opportunities in New York.
  D offer information about the eating habits of people in New York.

Big Apple al fresco

Scattered throughout the city of New York are dozens of 'secret' gardens, quiet corners, terraces and rooftops where you can escape the urban rush and dine amidst trees and flowering plants.

A TAVERN ON THE GREEN

Some call it a tourist trap, but the architecture and woodland setting guarantee a long and healthy life for this Central Park restaurant. Dinner in the garden on a summer's night, wrapped in the scent of a thousand flowers and lit by Japanese lanterns, is truly an affair to remember. And the extravagant desserts are a luscious way to celebrate a birthday or other special occasion.

B BOATHOUSE CAFÉ

While tourists are queuing up for tables at Tavern on the Green, New Yorkers head deeper into Central Park for lunch at this charming, relatively inexpensive café. The main attraction here is the setting, which overlooks the park's Boathouse Pond with the skyscrapers of midtown in the ⫸→

background. The food at the Boathouse is admittedly unimpressive although you won't go wrong with the pasta dishes or burgers.

C COURTYARD CAFÉ & BAR

Located in the heart of midtown near Grand Central Terminal, this eatery in the Doral Court Hotel qualifies as one of New York's best-kept secrets. The garden here, though small, is one of the city's finest with umbrella-shaded tables next to a sparkling waterfall.

D AMERICAN FESTIVAL CAFÉ

'Golden Boy', the famous statue, oversees the festivities at this restaurant situated in the shadow of New York's Art Deco architectural masterpiece. In winter, the outdoor section of the café is transformed into the Rockefeller Center Skating Rink; in summer, the shaded, linen-draped tables make an inviting prospect after a hard morning of shopping.

E RIVER CAFÉ

New York City's best outdoor dining experience is across the Brooklyn Bridge at this boat-restaurant moored in the East River. In an informal survey, six out of seven New Yorkers picked the River Café as the best place in the city to propose marriage. Positive features: stunning views of the Manhattan skyline, and of picture-perfect sunsets; inventive contemporary cooking with an American accent.

F MANHATTAN CHILLI COMPANY

Outdoor cafés are thick on the ground in Greenwich Village – it's hardly worth recommending one, since visitors so quickly find their own. It's easy to walk by the Manhattan Chilli Company which looks like just another quaint Village restaurant from the street. Step inside, though, and you'll discover gigantic bowls of good chilli served in a peaceful garden.

G YAFFA CAFÉ

When the western half of Greenwich Village changed into a center for tourists, the area's artists and musicians moved east to the neighbourhood known as Alphabet City. For a glimpse of arty New York, 1990s style, take a seat in Yaffa's uniquely urban garden; order a plate of food and a pot of herb tea and watch the world go by.

H JOSEPHINA

An excellent position across the street from Lincoln Center for the Performing Arts draws diners to this exotic restaurant; the delicately seasoned recipes and fresher-than-fresh ingredients bring them back. Owner/chef Louis Lanza uses flavoured oils and fresh stocks to delight the taste-buds without excessive sugar or fat. (The exception: sinfully rich desserts. Shrugs Lanza, 'Nobody's perfect.') Josephina offers two outdoor options, a sidewalk café that's perfect for people-watching and a lushly landscaped back garden.

PAPER 2 WRITING (1 hour 30 minutes)

PART 1

*You **must** answer this question.*

1 Your friend has seen this job advertisement and is planning to apply. You
worked for the same company last year. Using the information in the
advertisement and the notes you have made on it, tell your friend what the job
was really like and give him or her any advice you think necessary.

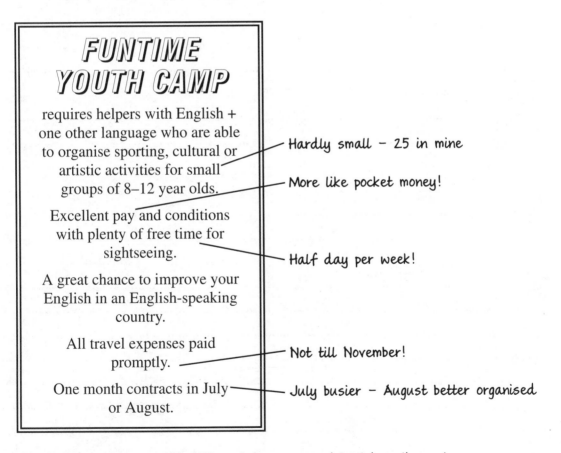

FUNTIME
YOUTH CAMP

requires helpers with English +
one other language who are able
to organise sporting, cultural or
artistic activities for small
groups of 8–12 year olds.

— *Hardly small – 25 in mine*

— *More like pocket money!*

Excellent pay and conditions
with plenty of free time for
sightseeing.

— *Half day per week!*

A great chance to improve your
English in an English-speaking
country.

All travel expenses paid
promptly.

— *Not till November!*

One month contracts in July
or August.

— *July busier – August better organised*

Write **a letter** of between **120–180** words in an appropriate style on the next
page. Do not write any addresses.

PART 1

PART 2

Write an answer to **one** *of the questions* **2–5** *in this part. Write your answer in* **120–180** *words in an appropriate style on the next page, putting the question number in the box.*

2   Your school magazine or company newsletter has decided to use its back page for a regular entertainment section. Write a **review** of a film or play you have seen recently, describing the film or play and saying why you would or would not recommend others to go and see it.

3   You see this notice in a magazine for learners of English, and decide to send in a story:

> We wish to publish a collection of stories from our readers, all with the title **The day that did most for my English**.
>
>   If you have an interesting or amusing story which you would like to share with others, please send it to us as soon as possible.

Write your **story** for the magazine.

4   Your teacher has asked you to describe some of the ways in which the place where you live has changed during your lifetime. Write a **description**, explaining whether these changes are for the better or the worse, and why you think this.

5   **Background reading texts**

Answer **one** of the following two questions based on your reading of **one** of the set books (see p.2). Write the title of the book next to the question number box.

Either   **(a)**   Describe any character or event in the book which you find improbable and explain why.

or   **(b)**   Describe the opening of the book and say whether it made you want to read the rest of the story. Explain why or why not.

PART 2

Question	

....

....

....

....

....

....

....

....

....

....

....

....

....

....

....

....

....

....

....

....

....

....

....

....

....

....

....

....

PAPER 3 USE OF ENGLISH (1 hour 15 minutes)

PART 1

For questions 1–15, read the text below and decide which answer A, B, C or D best fits each space. There is an example at the beginning (0).
Mark your answers **on the separate answer sheet.**

Example:

0   **A** in   **B** along   **C** up   **D** over

0	A	B	C	D
	—			

A VISITOR FOR MISS DREDGER

Every summer Miss Dredger took **(0)** .... visitors at Clôs de Joi. It was a square house with a **(1)** .... across the island to the sea, with the island of Jersey on the **(2)** .... .

Miss Dredger had **(3)** .... a carriage to take her down the harbour hill. **(4)** .... it was a steep descent, she would **(5)** .... have taken it in her purposeful stride, and would even have returned **(6)** .... foot up the long slope, for Miss Dredger scorned all physical **(7)** .... .

Nevertheless, she had **(8)** .... on a carriage this **(9)** .... morning, for she had a gentleman to meet at the harbour. Both he and his luggage must be got up the harbour hill. It was **(10)** .... that the luggage could not walk up on its own and from what she knew about men, it was ten **(11)** .... one that her new lodger **(12)** .... be as helpless as his luggage.

And so, as the carriage had to go down the hill before it could come up again, Miss Dredger, with her sharp **(13)** .... of logic, decided that, in order to **(14)** .... use of this fact, it would be as well to be **(15)** .... for at Clôs de Joi.

1 **A** sight   **B** vision   **C** view   **D** look

2 **A** distance   **B** background   **C** outskirts   **D** horizon

3 **A** ordered   **B** required   **C** commanded   **D** asked

4 **A** However   **B** Although   **C** Despite   **D** Even

5 **A** commonly   **B** actually   **C** mostly   **D** normally

6 **A** at   **B** on   **C** with   **D** off

7 **A** weakness   **B** lightness   **C** tenderness   **D** softness

8 **A** decided   **B** chosen   **C** arranged   **D** considered

9 **A** definite   **B** certain   **C** particular   **D** individual

10 **A** honest   **B** simple   **C** direct   **D** plain

11 **A** to   **B** by   **C** for   **D** under

12 **A** should   **B** would   **C** ought   **D** could

13 **A** sense   **B** idea   **C** feeling   **D** impression

14 **A** take   **B** have   **C** make   **D** get

15 **A** looked   **B** visited   **C** sent   **D** called

PART 2

*For questions **16–30**, read the text below and think of the word which best fits each space. Use only **one** word in each space. There is an example at the beginning (**0**).*
*Write your word **on the separate answer sheet**.*

Example:

0	*one*	0

THE HORSE IN ART

There is little doubt that **(0)** .... of the chief roles of the horse in art, just **(16)** .... in life, is that of our servant and companion. We can have very little idea of **(17)** .... a horse feels in its natural state. Left to itself, **(18)** .... is unlikely that it would pull a plough, take a soldier **(19)** .... a dangerous situation in battle, **(20)** .... do most of the other things that have attracted painters and writers to the animal ever **(21)** .... the dawn of history.

The horse is controlled **(22)** .... the wishes of its owner. When we describe it, we say it has **(23)** .... virtues and qualities we most admire in ourselves and it is as the symbol **(24)** .... these qualities that it has so often **(25)** .... praised by painters and poets. Then we must consider the horse's own beauty, speed and strength. **(26)** .... truth, the picture we **(27)** .... most frequently moved by, in both art and literature, is actually a single image that combines all the advantages of the animal and its rider. An outstanding example of **(28)** .... is provided by the school of sculpture and painting in **(29)** .... the authority and personality of individuals is emphasised by the **(30)** .... that they are on horseback.

PART 3

*For questions **31–40**, complete the second sentence so that it has a similar meaning to the first sentence, using the word given.* **Do not change the word given**. *You must use between two and five words, including the word given. There is an example at the beginning (**0**).*
*Write **only** the missing words **on the separate answer sheet**.*

Example:

0   I last saw him at my 21st birthday party.
   since

   I .... my 21st birthday party.

The gap can be filled by the words 'haven't seen him since' so you write:

0	*haven't seen him since*	0	0 1 2

---

31 Do you know who this coat belongs to?
   coat

   Do you know .... is?

32 Jo's training accident meant she couldn't take part in the race.
   prevented

   Jo's training accident .... part in the race.

33 Cyclists are not allowed to ride on the station platform.
   must

   Bicycles .... on the station platform.

34 To Alan's amazement, the passport office was closed when he arrived.
   find

   Alan .... the passport office closed when he arrived.

35 It isn't necessary to book tickets for the show in advance.
   need

   You .... tickets for the show in advance.

36 The top shelf was so high that the children couldn't reach it.
high

The top shelf was .... the children to reach.

37 I'd prefer you to start work next week.
rather

I .... work next week.

38 'Do you remember what you have to do?' the teacher asked her class.
what

The teacher asked her class if .... to do.

39 It's unusual for Carol to get angry with her staff.
hardly

Carol .... temper with her staff.

40 There is no ice-cream left.
run

We .... ice-cream.

PART 4

*For questions **41–55**, read the text below and look carefully at each line. Some of the lines are correct, and some have a word which should not be there. If a line is correct, put a tick (✓) by the number **on the separate answer sheet**. If a line has a word which should **not** be there, write the word **on the separate answer sheet**. There are two examples at the beginning (**0** and **00**).*

Examples:

0	✓	0
00	*as*	0

A LETTER OF APOLOGY

Dear Richard,

0   Thanks very much for your letter. It was good to hear

00   all your news and I'm glad that your family are all as well.

41   It's very kind of you to invite for me to stay with you in

42   the June, but unfortunately my final exams are that month

43   and I don't yet know of the dates. I think they may be in

44   the week that you've suggested. In any case, judging

45   from my last Geography results, I will need to be studying

46   rather more than having a good time with my friends.

47   As soon as I will get the dates, I'll let you know but I

48   don't much expect I'll be able to come. Perhaps we'll be

49   able to get something organised for July. It's a long time

50   ever since we got together and I'd love to catch up on

51   what has been happening to you. If only your parents

52   don't want their house full of visitors in the holiday, you

53   could come over to stay with me. There's a plenty of

54   room and the house is just at a short bike ride from the

55   beach, so there would be lots to do. Let me know it if you

think this is a good idea.

Best wishes

PART 5

For questions **56–65**, read the text below. Use the word given in capitals at the end of each line to form a word that fits in the space in the same line. There is an example at the beginning (**0**). Write your word **on the separate answer sheet**.

Example:

0	*natural*	0

AN IMPORTANT ENGLISH TOWN

The site of the town of Winchester was a **(0)** .... place for a | **NATURE**
(56) .... , at the point where a river cut through the chalk of the | **SETTLE**
(57) .... hillsides. A simple camp at St Catherine's Hill was the | **SOUTH**
(58) .... known use of the site. This was followed by an Iron Age | **EARLY**
hill-fort, but this was left **(59)** .... by 100 BC. It was the Romans who | **INHABIT**
finally established the town and **(60)** .... it with a defensive wall for | **ROUND**
the protection of their people and trade.

With the **(61)** .... of its first cathedral in the seventh century, the | **BUILD**
town became an important **(62)** .... centre. Later, King Alfred, who | **RELIGION**
had **(63)** .... pushed back the invading Danes, moved his palace | **SUCCESS**
to Winchester. The town then experienced rapid **(64)** .... , and | **DEVELOP**
its **(65)** .... role in English history was underlined in 1066 when the | **CENTRE**
conquering Normans, like Alfred, made Winchester their capital.

PAPER 4   LISTENING (approximately 40 minutes)

PART 1

You will hear people talking in eight different situations.
*For questions **1–8**, choose the best answer, **A**, **B** or **C**.*

1 You are walking round a market when you hear this woman talking to a customer.
What is she doing?

   A asking the customer's opinion

   B offering a cheap sample

   C explaining a price rise

                        1

2 You're in the doctor's waiting room when you overhear the nurse on the phone.
Why didn't she send off the notes?

   A She didn't know they were wanted.

   B It isn't part of her job to do it.

   C She didn't know which notes to send.

                        2

3 You're in a gallery when you hear these women talking.
What are they looking at?

   A a bowl

   B a lamp

   C a vase

                        3

4 You are visiting a large company and you hear two people talking.
What are they discussing?

   A a personal computer

   B a typewriter

   C a CD player

                        4

5 Listen to this clerk at a station booking office.
Which is the cheapest ticket?

A a period return

B an ordinary return

C a Rover

	5

6 These friends are talking about a film.
Who will go to see it?

A both of them

B neither of them

C the girl

	6

7 These people are talking about a colleague.
What's his problem?

A His boss is unfair to him.

B He has been ill.

C He has too much to do.

	7

8 Listen to this woman phoning a travel agent.
What does she want to do?

A cancel her booking

B postpone her holiday

C change her destination

	8

PART 2

You will hear an interview about sports facilities.
*For questions **9–18**, fill in the answers on the questionnaire.*

Where does the interviewee live?	9
What is the interviewee's occupation?	10
How often does s/he use a public swimming pool?	11
What does s/he feel about the opening times?	12
What about entry charges?	13
What does s/he feel about existing facilities?	14
What would s/he most like to see added to these?	15
What other sports should be catered for locally?	16
Where should money for improvements come from?	17
Who should be able to use the pool free?	18

PART 3

You will hear five people talking to someone they have just met.
For questions **19–23**, choose which of the people **A–F** each speaker is talking to.
Use the letters only once. There is one extra letter which you do not need to use.

A   a tenant

B   a neighbour

C   a holidaymaker

D   a colleague at work

E   a trainee

F   a hotel guest

Speaker 1	19
Speaker 2	20
Speaker 3	21
Speaker 4	22
Speaker 5	23

PART 4

You will hear a discussion between Andy and Sharon about advertising their small business.

*For questions **24–30**, decide which of the statements are true and which are false and write **T** for True or **F** for False in the box provided.*

24 They have decided to spend some money on advertising.

	24

25 Their customers found their last advertisement boring.

	25

26 They need to attract better staff.

	26

27 Andy has contacted the local newspaper.

	27

28 They agree to advertise once a week.

	28

29 Sharon thinks a professional delivery company would cost too much.

	29

30 Andy agrees they should employ students.

	30

PAPER 5   SPEAKING (approximately 15 minutes)

Part 1

You tell the examiner about yourself. The examiner may ask you questions such as: Where are you from? How do you usually spend your free time? What are your plans for the future? Your partner does the same.

Part 2

The examiner gives you two pictures to look at and asks you to talk about them for about a minute. Your partner does the same with two different pictures.

Part 3

The examiner gives you a photograph or drawing to look at with your partner. You are asked to solve a problem or come to a decision about something in the picture. For example, you might be asked to decide the best way to use some rooms in a language school. You discuss the problem together.

Part 4

You are asked more questions connected with your discussion in Part 3. For example, you might be asked to talk about the best ways of studying.

Practice Test 3

PAPER 1   READING (1 hour 15 minutes)

PART 1

*You are going to read a newspaper article about women and technical subjects.
Choose from the list (**A–I**) the sentence which best summarises each part (**1–7**) of
the article. There is one extra sentence which you do not need to use. There is an
example at the beginning (**0**).*
Mark your answers **on the separate answer sheet**.

A	Women often can't find, or don't think of looking for, the opportunities they need.
B	Women are needed in jobs that require a technological background.
C	Women study basic subjects alongside more specialised ones.
D	At the end of the course, women usually find jobs in local industry.
E	Women who want to change their jobs cannot because they have the wrong qualifications.
F	It is difficult to convince women and girls that they should take up scientific subjects.
G	In one training centre, the women are very eager to study scientific and technological subjects.
H	It is often difficult to obtain a place on a course.
I	My early interests were not developed.

Workface

A second chance to pick up a screwdriver, plug into the future and join the enthusiasts back at school

0	*I*

'I'VE always been interested in electronics and I often opened up the TV or the hi-fi to have a look. But I wasn't encouraged at school; I was the only girl in the Physics class and I felt lonely and depressed.'

1	

Susan Veerasamie's experience is typical of many. Eager to be the same as their friends, teenage girls shy away from technical and science subjects at school and then after a few years in a low-paid dead-end, 'woman's' job, they find they haven't got the qualifications to enable them to change course.

2	

The Haringey Women's Training and Education Centre, which Susan Veerasamie attends, is one of a handful of centres offering women a second chance to study technological and engineering subjects. It is housed in part of a former secondary school in north London and I doubt that the building has ever seen such keen students.

3	

The Centre provides courses in electronics, computing, the construction trades and science and technical skills, and everyone attends classes in numeracy, English and business practice.

4	

Hopefully, when they have completed their courses, the Centre's students will have gained enough confidence and basic skills to find a job or go on to further study. Nevertheless, getting on to a course at a college of further education is not easy if you don't have the required qualifications. The Manpower Services Commission offers courses in craft and technological skills which are open to everyone who is unemployed. However, places are often in high demand and the courses offered depend on the needs of local industry.

5	

There are other introductory and 'taster' courses similar to the Haringey Centre's around the country but they are scarce. It is often difficult for women to find a course that meets their needs and there is little to attract the attention of those who may never have considered work in the engineering and technological fields.

6	

The problem is how to persuade girls to broaden their options, and also to introduce training and retraining to women who have chosen more traditional paths, only to find the way to improved employment prospects closed or, at best, unsatisfying.

7	

Encouraging women to enter traditional 'male' work areas in greater numbers in this way is not only important for the women themselves, in that it offers a route into higher paid work, but it is also important for the country as a whole. There is a general skills shortage in the technological industries. We need these women's enthusiasm and ability.

*You are going to read an extract about children's fiction. For questions **8–15**, choose*
*the answer (**A, B, C** or **D**) which you think fits best according to the text.*
*Mark your answers **on the separate answer sheet**.*

What is good writing for children?

The children's publishers will tell you they look for 'good writing'. What exactly do they mean?

Before you send a story you have written to any publisher at all, your severest critic ought to be you yourself. To have a chance of succeeding in the competitive market of children's fiction, you should constantly be aware, every single time you sit down at your word-processor, of the need to produce 'good, original writing'. A difficult task, maybe, but one which hopefully we will help you to achieve.

To begin with, let us try to pin down exactly what publishers mean when they talk about 'good writing' for children. A useful starting point would be to take a look at some of the children's books which won literary prizes last year. Reading these books is one of the easiest and most enjoyable ways of: (a) finding out what individual publishers are publishing at the moment, and (b) learning a few tricks of the trade from well-established professionals. It goes without saying, of course, that slavishly copying the style and subject matter of a successful author is usually a recipe for disaster. Nor should you become downhearted after reading a particularly brilliant piece of work, and miserably think you will never be able to match up to those standards. Remember, overnight success is rare – most successful children's authors will have struggled long and hard to learn their trade. Read these books as a critic; note down the things you enjoyed or admired, as well as areas where you feel there was possibly room for improvement. After all, nobody is perfect, not even a successful, prize-winning author.

Possibly the toughest challenge is right at the youngest end of the age range – the picture book. The would-be author/illustrator is attempting to create an exciting story out of the narrow, limited, everyday world of a young child's experience – not easy at all. The whole storyline has to be strong enough to keep the reader turning the pages, yet simple enough to fit into a few pages. Another problem for the new picture-book author is that it can seem that every subject and every approach has been done to death, with nothing new left to say. Add to this the fact that printing costs are high because of full colour illustrations, which means that the publisher will probably want a text that suits the international market to increase sales, and a novel for ten-year olds, with hardly any pictures at all, starts to look much more inviting.

You would be forgiven for wondering if there are any truly original plots left to impress publishers with. But remember that, in many ways, it is the writer's own personal style, and intelligent handling of a subject that can change a familiar, overworked plot into something original and fresh. To illustrate this, read *The Enchanted Horse* by Magdalen Nabb. A young girl called Irina finds an old wooden horse in a junk shop, takes it home and treats it as if it was real. Soon it magically starts to come to life … Sounds familiar? The magic object that comes alive is a storyline that has been used in hundreds of other children's stories. So why does it succeed here? The answer is that Magdalen Nabb has created a strong, believable character in the lonely, unhappy heroine Irina, and the descriptions of her relationship with the wooden horse are poetic and touching.

So, to return to the question asked at the beginning: What exactly is 'good writing' for children? The answer is that it is writing which is fresh, exciting and unpredictable, and which gives a new and original angle on what might be a well-worn subject. But do not be put off if you feel that you simply cannot match up to all these requirements. While there is obviously no substitute for talent, and the ability to come up with suitable ideas, many of the techniques for improving and polishing your manuscript can be learned.

Visual materials for Paper 5

1A

1B

2A

2B

1C

1D

2C

2D

1E

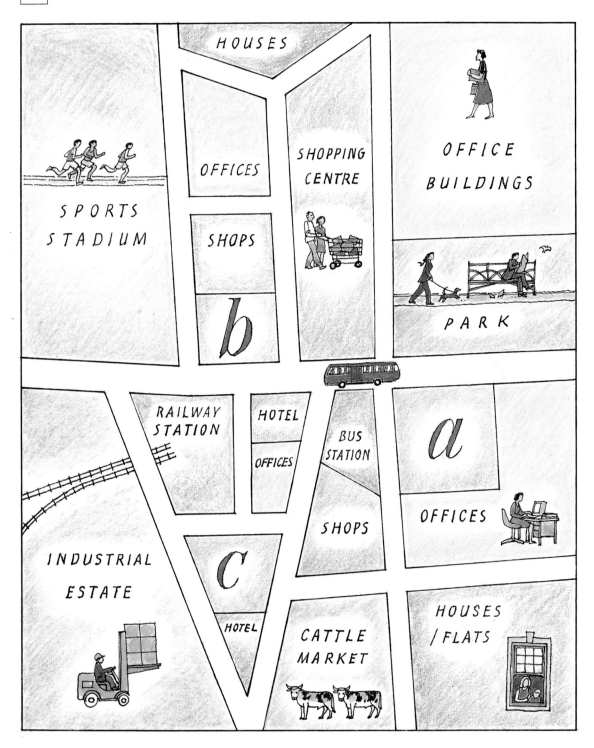

2E

Gifts for all!

2F

 Miguel

 Julia

 Tom

 Helen

4E

3A

3B

4A

4B

3C

3D

4C

4D

3E

Success in sport

talent

unlimited money

lots of practice

sympathetic family

good equipment/facilities

professional coaching

8 Why does the article advise people to look at prize-winning books?
  A to copy the author's style
  B to realise what a high standard needs to be reached
  C to get an idea of what might be successful
  D to find out how to trick publishers

9 What do most successful children's authors have in common?
  A They did not get depressed by early failures.
  B They have learned how to be critical of other authors' work.
  C They find it easy to think of storylines that will sell.
  D They have worked hard to become well-known.

10 Why is the picture book the most difficult to write?
  A There is a limited range of subjects available.
  B Young children cannot follow storylines easily.
  C The pictures need to be exciting.
  D Children want to be able to read it quickly.

11 What looks 'more inviting' in line 54?
  A the international market
  B the increased sales
  C the novel for ten-year-olds
  D the type of pictures

12 The book about Irina is successful
  A because of the unusual way magic is used.
  B because of the way the character is described.
  C because the story has not been told before.
  D because the pictures bring the story to life.

13 What does 'it' refer to in line 68?
  A the storyline
  B the magic object
  C the horse
  D the children's story

14 What conclusion does the writer of the text come to?
  A Anyone can learn to write a good story.
  B The subject matter is the most important consideration.
  C If you have natural ability, you can learn the rest.
  D Some published fiction is badly written.

15 Why was this text written?
  A to explain what kind of books children like to read
  B to give advice to people who want to write children's fiction
  C to discourage new authors from being too optimistic
  D to persuade new authors to get away from old ideas

PART 3

You are going to read a magazine article about bodyclocks. Seven sentences have been removed from the article. Choose from the sentences (A–H) the one which fits each gap (16–21). There is one extra sentence which you do not need to use. There is an example at the beginning (0).
Mark your answers on the separate answer sheet.

RHYTHM
OF LIFE

Scientists have discovered that our bodies operate on a 25-hour day. So tuning into your bodyclock can make things really tick, says Jenny Hope, *Daily Mail* Medical Correspondent.

Choosing the right time to sleep, the correct moment to make decisions, the best hour to eat – and even go into hospital – could be your key to perfect health.

Centuries after man discovered the rhythms of the planets and the cycles of crops, scientists have learned that we too live by precise rhythms that govern the ebb and flow of everything from our basic bodily functions to mental skills. **0** | *H* |

But it's not just the experts who are switching on to the way our bodies work. **16** | | Prince Charles consults a chart which tells him when he will be at his peak on a physical, emotional and intellectual level. Boxer Frank Bruno is another who charts his bio-rhythms to plan for big fights.

17 | | Sleep, blood pressure, hormone levels and heartbeat all follow their own clocks, which may bear only slight relation to our man-made 24-hour cycle.

Research shows that in laboratory experiments when social signals and, most crucially, light indicators such as dawn are taken away, people lose touch with the 24-hour clock and sleeping patterns change. **18** | |

In the real world, light and dark keep adjusting internal clocks to the 24-hour day. **19** | | As it falls from a 10 p.m. high of 37.2°C to a pre-dawn low of 36.1°C, mental functions fall too. This is a key reason why shift work can cause so many problems – both for workers and their organisations.

20 | | The three operators in the control room worked alternating weeks of day, evening and night shifts – a dangerous combination which never gave their bodies' natural rhythms a chance to settle down. Investigators believe this caused the workers to over-look a warning light and fail to close an open valve.

Finding the secret of what makes us tick has long fascinated scientists and work done over the last decade has yielded important clues.

21 [ ] For example, the time we eat may be important if we want to maximise intellectual or sporting performance. There is already evidence suggesting that the time when medicine is given to patients affects how well it works.

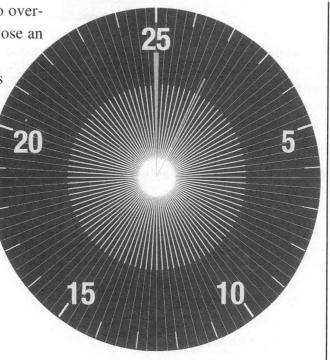

A   Temperature and heartbeat cycles lengthen and settle into 'days' lasting about 25 hours.

B   The most famous example is the nuclear accident at Three Mile Island in the US.

C   But the best indicator of performance is body temperature.

D   Leading experts say every aspect of human biology is influenced by daily rhythms.

E   Dr Michael Stroud is one of the few people alive who can genuinely claim to have tested their bodyclocks to the limit.

F   The aim is to help us become more efficient.

G   An increasing number of people study the state of their bio-rhythms before making their daily plans.

H   Man is a prisoner of time.

PART 4

You are going to read about four competitions which offer holidays as prizes. For questions **22–35**, choose from the competitions (**A–D**). Some of the competitions may be chosen more than once. When more than one answer is required, these may be given in any order. There is an example at the beginning (**0**).
Mark your answers **on the separate answer sheet**.

Which holiday prize offers you the chance to:

visit a desert?	**0**	*B*	
go to the seaside?	**22**		**23**
stay in a new hotel?	**24**		
have a chance to exercise?	**25**		**26**
be sure of seeing some animals?	**27**		
look around the city and see something of the countryside?	**28**		
stay longer than a week?	**29**		**30**

Which competition extract:

describes what will happen on the flight?	**31**
says there is more than one prize?	**32**
offers to take the winner on a historical tour as part of the prize	**33**
offers a holiday which includes all food?	**34**
is advertising a particular product?	**35**

A

clearly CANADA

Vancouver is a stylish, metropolitan centre with the scenic Pacific Ocean at its feet and impressive coastal mountains behind. To give you the chance to experience its delights for yourself, *Options* magazine has teamed up with 'Clearly Canadian' – a blend of native Canadian fruit flavours and sparkling water – to bring you this great competition.

The lucky prizewinner and guest will enjoy a fabulous ten-day getaway, flying direct to Vancouver with Canadian Airlines. On board, they will enjoy an in-flight movie while sampling a delicious meal served on real china.

Accommodation for the winner and guest will be at Shangri-La's Pacific Palisades Hotel, one of Vancouver's first-class hotels. They will enjoy a luxury executive suite, with stunning views over the harbour, and use of the hotel's health club and pool. Ten runners-up will receive a bottle of 'Clearly Canadian' and an exclusively designed T-shirt.

While in Vancouver, you will have many opportunities to sample Canadian city life. Browse in fashionable shops, linger in sidewalk cafés or relax on the beach.

Buy this magazine next week and we'll give you the competition details.

B

GO WILD!

NAMIBIA is a country of desert dunes, wide horizons and clear skies. Enter this competition and you and a friend could be on your way.

Your one-week prize holiday begins at Heathrow airport where you will board an Air Namibia plane bound for the capital. Air Namibia Holidays' magnificent Namibia tour will take you straight to the very heart of the country. All travel arrangements will be taken care of – all you have to do is sit back and enjoy the scenery. You'll start with a drive to the Namib Desert Park, then go on to see the pelicans, flamingos and terns at Walvis Bay lagoon, before heading for the coastal resort of Swakopmund.

The highlight of the tour is a safari through Etosha National Park, home to thousands of elephants, zebras, giraffes and antelopes as well as lions, leopards, cheetahs and rhinos.

All meals are included throughout the holiday and you'll stay in some of Namibia's best lodges and camps.

We just ask you to think of

C

WIN A FABULOUS HOLIDAY FOR TWO!

Visit the deserted city of Fatehpur Sikri. Stand back in amazement as you marvel at the wildlife reserves where you'll see exotic birds and possibly even a tiger! These are just some of the sights you'll experience on the thrilling ten-day 'Moghul Highlights' holiday.

The holiday begins with a tour of Old Delhi. Proceeding by road to Agra, you'll stop on the way to see the Tomb of Akbar. Moving on to see Agra Fort and the beautiful Taj Mahal on the banks of the Yamuna River, your group will then explore Akbar's red sandstone city, Fatehpur Sikri, built in 1574. Lunch will be taken in the Keoladeo National Park at Bharatpur, a birdwatcher's paradise.

This fantastic holiday package includes the return flight from Heathrow to Delhi, the holiday tour and insurance. All breakfasts while in India are included but holiday participants will need to buy meals at local restaurants in India.

To find out what you have to do

D

win *a week of luxury in* BUDAPEST

The lucky winner and a friend will fly direct to Budapest International Airport and will then be taken to The Palace Hotel, a luxurious hotel set in its own large park on the banks of the river Danube. The Palace Hotel is just two years old – a modern addition to the ancient skyline.

You'll enjoy five nights' bed and breakfast accommodation in a room that overlooks the river Danube, and will be treated to dinner in the Café Suisse. We have not ordered lunch for you but it is also available in the restaurant.

The week in Budapest can be spent at leisure either relaxing in the hotel and its grounds, or wandering around the superb shopping arcade. Alternatively, The Palace Hotel has extensive health club facilities – including an indoor pool and a free steam bath. If you're feeling really energetic, you could play a game of tennis or jog around the grounds on the two-mile landscaped track.

To make sure you take in some of the sights of Budapest, you may wish to book at very reasonable cost a day's sightseeing with President Holidays.

Look at the next page to see what you have to do.

PAPER 2   WRITING (1 hour 30 minutes)

PART 1

*You **must** answer this question.*

1   You are on holiday at the Bayview Hotel and have decided to come back to the same place next year. You have kept a diary during your stay. Part of this is shown below with the holiday advertisement which you cut out. You have made some notes on the advertisement.

Read the diary and the advertisement. Then write a letter to your friend, persuading him or her to come with you next year. Use the information given to say what you could do together.

MONDAY

Sailing – first time for me!

Evening – new Spielberg film

TUESDAY

Coach trip to old town

Evening – disco

Bayview Hotel
Family-run hotel on sea front. Restaurant, bars.

friendly people   *good food*

Write a letter of between **120–180** words in an appropriate style on the next page. Do not write any addresses.

PART 1

PART 2

*Write an answer to **one** of the questions **2–5** in this part. Write your answer in
120–180 words in an appropriate style on the next page, putting the question
number in the box.*

2   As part of a new series, an educational magazine has invited readers to write
    articles called **How and why I started learning English**. Write an **article**
    based on your own experience.

3   Your teacher has asked you to write a story which includes the sentence **That
    was the moment when I realised I was in the wrong place**. Write your
    story.

4   A local newspaper has invited reviews of restaurants from its readers. Write a
    report on a visit to **one** local restaurant. Your report should cover the food,
    service, decoration and atmosphere of the restaurant, and should also
    comment on any problems you experienced.

5   **Background reading texts**

    Answer **one** of the following two questions based on your reading of **one** of
    the set books (see p.2). Write the title of the book next to the question number
    box.

    Either **(a)**   Describe some of the most important actions in the book and
                explain how they help to develop the story.
    or   **(b)**   Would the book make a good film? Say why or why not.

PART 2

Question	

....
....
....
....
....
....
....
....
....
....
....
....
....
....
....
....
....
....
....
....
....
....
....
....
....
....
....
....
....
....
....

PAPER 3   USE OF ENGLISH (1 hour 15 minutes)

PART 1

For questions 1–15, read the text below and decide which answer A, B, C or D best fits each space. There is an example at the beginning (0).
Mark your answers on the separate answer sheet.

Example:
0   **A** sigh   **B** yawn   **C** cough   **D** sneeze

0	A	B	C	D
	▬	▭	▭	▭

HELEN AND MARTIN

With a thoughtful **(0)** .... , Helen turned away from the window and walked back to her favourite armchair. **(1)** .... her brother never arrive? For a brief moment, she wondered if she really cared that much.

Over the years Helen had given **(2)** .... waiting for Martin to take an interest in her. Her feelings for him had gradually **(3)** .... until now, as she sat waiting for him, she experienced no more than a sister's **(4)** .... to see what had **(5)** .... of her brother.

Almost without **(6)** .... , Martin had lost his job with a busy publishing company after spending the last eight years in New York as a key figure in the US office. Somehow the two of them hadn't **(7)** .... to keep in touch and, left alone, Helen had slowly found her **(8)** .... in her own judgement growing. **(9)** .... the wishes of her parents, she had left university halfway **(10)** .... her course and now, to the astonishment of the whole family, she was **(11)** .... a fast-growing reputation in the pages of respected art magazines and was actually earning enough to live **(12)** .... from her paintings.

Of course, she **(13)** .... no pleasure in Martin's sudden misfortune, but she couldn't **(14)** .... looking forward to her brother's arrival with **(15)** .... satisfaction at what she had achieved.

1 **A** Could   **B** Should   **C** Would   **D** Ought

2 **A** in   **B** up   **C** out   **D** away

3 **A** depressed   **B** weakened   **C** lowered   **D** fainted

4 **A** wonder   **B** idea   **C** curiosity   **D** regard

5 **A** become   **B** developed   **C** arisen   **D** changed

6 **A** caution   **B** warning   **C** advice   **D** signal

7 **A** minded   **B** concerned   **C** worried   **D** bothered

8 **A** dependence **B** confidence   **C** certainty   **D** courage

9 **A** Ignoring   **B** Omitting   **C** Avoiding   **D** Preventing

10 **A** along   **B** down   **C** through   **D** across

11 **A** gaining   **B** reaching   **C** starting   **D** opening

12 **A** for   **B** by   **C** with   **D** on

13 **A** made   **B** took   **C** drew   **D** formed

14 **A** help   **B** miss   **C** fail   **D** drop

15 **A** soft   **B** fine   **C** quiet   **D** still

PART 2

*For questions **16–30**, read the text below and think of the word which best fits each space. Use only **one** word in each space. There is an example at the beginning (**0**).*
*Write your word **on the separate answer sheet**.*

Example: | **0** | *most* | **0** |

CYCLING ROUND CORNERS

Taking a corner is one of the **(0)** .... satisfying moves you can make on a bike. It's fun, it's exciting, and it also happens **(16)** .... be one of the hardest things to learn. Even **(17)** .... experienced rider can always **(18)** .... improvements in this area. Good cornering is the ability to cycle through a turn **(19)** .... full control, no matter **(20)** .... the conditions. This might mean racing **(21)** .... high speed down a winding descent, but just **(22)** .... important is the ability to deal with a slow, sharp turn **(23)** .... you are touring with lots of luggage. In **(24)** .... these cases there are some general points to remember.

When going very slowly you can steer through a corner using your hands on the handlebars **(25)** .... , as speed increases, any sudden turning of the front wheel **(26)** .... likely to result in loss of control. To avoid **(27)** .... effect, a bike must be turned by leaning it, by steering with the body instead of the hands. On sharp turns of more **(28)** .... about 70 degrees, even this is **(29)** .... enough: you must also lower your body towards the bike as much as you **(30)** .... to help keep it from slipping out from under you. When you are cornering correctly you will feel very solid. It's a good feeling – exciting but not really dangerous.

PART 3

*For questions **31–40**, complete the second sentence so that it has a similar meaning to the first sentence, using the word given. **Do not change the word given**. You must use between two and five words, including the word given. There is an example at the beginning (**0**).*
*Write **only** the missing words **on the separate answer sheet**.*

Example:

0   I last saw him at my 21st birthday party.
   since

   I .... my 21st birthday party.

The gap can be filled by the words 'haven't seen him since' so you write:

0	*haven't seen him since*	0	0 1 2

31 There's no point in asking George to help.
   worth

   It .... George to help.

32 Harry couldn't get his parents' permission to buy a motorbike.
   let

   Harry's parents .... a motorbike.

33 'Where have I left my sunglasses, David?' asked Susan.
   where

   Susan asked David .... sunglasses.

34 John's behaviour at the party annoyed me.
   John

   I was annoyed by the .... at the party.

35 It's a good thing you lent me the money or I would have had to go to the bank.
   you

   I would have had to go to the bank .... me the money.

36 Matthew didn't listen to what his doctor told him.
notice

Matthew took .... advice.

37 Sheila had to finish the accounts and write several letters as well.
addition

Sheila had to finish the accounts .... several letters.

38 When he was a child in Australia, Mark went swimming almost every day.
his

Mark went swimming almost every day .... in Australia.

39 Let's visit the museum this afternoon.
go

Why .... the museum this afternoon?

40 Valerie found it hard to concentrate on her book because of the noise.
difficulty

Valerie .... her book because of the noise.

PART 4

For questions **41–55**, read the text below and look carefully at each line. Some of the lines are correct, and some have a word which should not be there. If a line is correct, put a tick (✓) by the number **on the separate answer sheet**. If a line has a word which should **not** be there, write the word **on the separate answer sheet**. There are two examples at the beginning (**0** and **00**).

Examples:

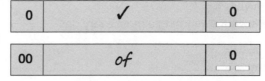

| 0 | ✓ | 0 |
| 00 | *of* | 0 |

A PLACE WORTH VISITING

0	The Welsh National Folk Museum in Cardiff is one of the
00	most interesting of places I've ever visited and it's situated in
41	a very pretty countryside. The museum has collected various
42	buildings from all over the country and brought them together
43	in the grounds of a historic manor house, near where they have
44	been carefully rebuilt one brick by brick to look just like they
45	did in their original position. Then the interiors they have
46	been furnished in period style, and many interesting old tools
47	and other everyday household objects are on the display
48	in this realistic setting. It's fascinating to walk away from
49	building to building, imagining about the way people used to
50	live since years ago. Large families often lived in the tiniest
51	of cottages, sometimes even sharing in the space with the
52	domestic animals which were of such an importance to them.
53	You can go around the manor house as well, but in my opinion
54	there is no little to distinguish this from many other historic
55	houses elsewhere. It does have a much comfortable tea-room,
	however, which is very welcome after all that walking.

PART 5

For questions **56–65**, read the text below. Use the word given in capitals at the end of each line to form a word that fits in the space in the same line. There is an example at the beginning (**0**). Write your word **on the separate answer sheet**.

Example:

0	*construction*	0

THE FUTURE OF TALL BUILDINGS

Architects responsible for the **(0)** .... of many skyscrapers believe   **CONSTRUCT**
that a tall building must always have a certain minimum **(56)** .... but   **WIDE**
that there is no limit to its absolute **(57)** .... . This means that the   **HIGH**
skyscrapers of the future are likely to be even taller.

Engineers agree with this, but there is **(58)** .... over the best shape for   **AGREE**
very tall, slim buildings. The effects of wind **(59)** .... mean that   **PRESS**
cylindrical designs have enjoyed some **(60)** .... in recent years, and   **POPULAR**
these are quite pleasing to the eye. **(61)** .... , however, the ideal   **FORTUNATE**
shape is an ugly square with heavily rounded corners.

Would these tall buildings of the future offer more than a **(62)** ....   **WONDER**
view? Some believe tall towers could contain all the **(63)** .... for   **REQUIRE**
modern living. The **(64)** .... of these vertical villages would travel up   **INHABIT**
and down between their home and work zones and would **(65)** ....   **RARE**
need to journey to ground level.

PAPER 4 LISTENING (approximately 40 minutes)

PART 1

You will hear people talking in eight different situations.
*For questions **1–8**, choose the best answer **A, B** or **C**.*

1 You are visiting a trade exhibition when you hear a speaker at one of the stands.
What is he demonstrating?

    A a watch

    B a lock

    C a burglar alarm

	1

2 This girl is talking about a party.
What was it like?

    A boring

    B too crowded

    C noisy

	2

3 Listen to this hotel receptionist talking on the phone.
Who is she talking to?

    A a friend

    B a guest

    C her employer

	3

4 You hear this advertisement on the radio.
Who is it aimed at?

    A people who have plenty of money

    B people who might borrow money

    C people who need to save money

	4

5 Listen to these students talking about their holiday work.
Where are they working?

    A   a library

    B   an office

    C   a shop

	5

6 Listen to this man.
Where has he been?

    A   to the gym

    B   to the dentist

    C   to the barber

	6

7 You hear this woman talking on the radio.
What is she discussing?

    A   music

    B   a picture

    C   architecture

	7

8 You hear this man talking to a shop assistant.
Why is he annoyed?

    A   His pen has leaked in his pocket.

    B   HIs pen has been repaired recently.

    C   His pen was very expensive.

	8

PART 2

You will hear a teacher telling new students about their course.
*For questions **9–18**, listen to what she says and complete the notes.*

Classes in Studio every afternoon

Room 51 on [9]

On Fridays can use [10] for private study

Extra courses: Monday [11]

Tuesday [12]

Wednesday [13]

Application forms from [14]

Saturday course on computer-aided design

Open to [15] students only

Must provide own [16]

Short absences, phone [17]

More than two days, write to [18]

PART 3

.You will hear five people saying thank you.
*For questions **19–23**, choose which of **A–F** each speaker is talking about. Use the*
letters only once. There is one extra letter which you do not need to use.

A good teaching

B support in a difficult task

Speaker 1		**19**
Speaker 2		**20**
Speaker 3		**21**
Speaker 4		**22**
Speaker 5		**23**

C a warning

D a present

E a piece of information

F a loan

PART 4

You will hear a radio discussion about a wildlife park.
*For questions 24–30, decide which of the choices **A, B** or **C** is the correct answer.*

24   Where is South Glen?

    A   inside Glenside Park
    B   between the park and the main road
    C   near the park

	24

25   What does Ian say about Helen's plans?

    A   He doesn't like them.
    B   He doesn't understand them.
    C   He doesn't know what they are.

	25

26   Helen claims that, at present, visitors

    A   walk about in large groups.
    B   go all over the park.
    C   damage the plants.

	26

27   Why is it a problem for the staff to raise young birds?

    A   They lack the necessary skills.
    B   It costs a lot of money.
    C   There isn't the right equipment.

	27

28   Ian thinks it is ridiculous to

    A   encourage more visitors.
    B   make visitors pay an entrance fee.
    C   build fences round the animals.

	28

29   Helen says that fires

    A   have been started by accident.
    B   are impossible to control.
    C   are a possible danger.

	29

30   Ian believes that the villagers nowadays

    A   are more aware of the environment than
        their grandparents.
    B   show enough respect for the environment.
    C   have become careless about the environment.

	30

PAPER 5   SPEAKING (approximately 15 minutes)

Part 1

You tell the examiner about yourself. The examiner may ask you questions such as: Where are you from? How do you usually spend your free time? What are your plans for the future? Your partner does the same.

Part 2

The examiner gives you two pictures to look at and asks you to talk about them for about a minute. Your partner does the same with two different pictures.

Part 3

The examiner gives you a photograph or drawing to look at with your partner. You are asked to solve a problem or come to a decision about something in the picture. For example, you might be asked to decide the best way to use some rooms in a language school. You discuss the problem together.

Part 4

You are asked more questions connected with your discussion in Part 3. For example, you might be asked to talk about the best ways of studying.

Practice Test 4

PAPER 1   READING (1 hour 15 minutes)

PART 1

*You are going to read a magazine article about pollution of the atmosphere. Choose the most suitable heading from the list (**A–I**) for each part (**1–7**) of the article. There is one extra heading which you do not need to use. There is an example at the beginning (**0**).*
*Mark your answers **on the separate answer sheet.***

A	Before ozone existed
B	Repair gets slower
C	People ignore warnings
D	Ozone hole a certainty
E	The future is our responsibility
F	The function of the ozone layer
G	Delayed reactions
H	Humans to blame
I	Strange results

The ozone layer
What is it? What is happening to it?

0	*I*

In September 1982, Dr Joe Farman, a British scientist working in the Antarctic, found that a dramatic change had taken place in the atmosphere above his research station on the ice continent. His instruments, set up to measure the amounts of a chemical called ozone in the atmosphere, seemed to go wild. Over just a few days they recorded that half the ozone had disappeared.

1	

He couldn't believe his eyes, so he came back to Britain to get a new instrument to check his findings. But when he returned the following year at the same time, the same thing happened. He had discovered a hole in the ozone layer – an invisible shield in the upper atmosphere – that turned out to extend over an area of the sky as wide as the United States and as deep as Mount Everest is high. When he published his findings in scientific journals, they caused a sensation. Scientists blamed pollution for causing the ozone hole.

2	

The ozone layer is between 15 and 40 kilometres up in the atmosphere, higher than most aeroplanes fly. This region contains most of the atmosphere's ozone, which is a special form of the gas oxygen. Ozone has the unique ability to stop certain dangerous invisible rays from the sun from reaching the Earth's surface – rather like a pair of sunglasses filters out bright sunlight. These rays are known as ultra-violet radiation. This damages living cells, causing sunburn and more serious diseases. The ozone layer is vital to life on the surface of the Earth.

3	

Until the ozone layer formed, about two thousand million years ago, it was impossible for any living thing to survive on the surface of the planet. All life was deep in the oceans. But once oxygen was formed in the air, and some of that oxygen turned to ozone, plants and animals could begin to move on to land.

4	

But now humans are damaging the ozone layer for the first time. In the past ten years, scientists have discovered that some man-made gases, used in everything from refrigerators and aerosols to fire extinguishers, are floating up into the ozone layer and destroying the ozone. The most common of these gases are called chlorofluorocarbons (CFCs).

5	

The damage is worst over Antarctica, and near the North Pole, where scientists have seen small holes appear for a short time each spring since 1989. So far, these holes have healed up again within a few weeks by natural processes in the atmosphere that create more ozone. But each year, it seems to take longer for the healing to be completed. Also, all round the planet, there now seems to be less ozone in the ozone layer than even a few years ago.

6	

The first new international law to stop people making or using CFCs was the Montreal Protocol, agreed by most of the world's governments in 1987. Since then, there have been new controls on other chemicals that destroy ozone. The problem is that it takes roughly eight years for CFCs, which are released when an old fridge is broken up, to reach the ozone layer. That is why, despite all the cuts, ozone holes were deeper than ever around both the North and South Poles in 1993. Amounts of CFCs in the atmosphere will continue to rise for another five years, say scientists.

7	

Every year, the atmosphere will attempt to repair damage to the ozone layer caused by our pollution. But we are stretching its capacity to recover to the limit. If we stop using all ozone-destroying chemicals within the next five years, it is likely to be at least the middle of the 21st century before the ozone hole stops forming over Antarctica each year. And, if we are to survive, we all have to face the problem now.

PART 2

You are going to read an article about a woman called Rebecca Ridgway. For questions **8–14**, choose the answer (**A, B, C** or **D**) which you think fits best according to the text.

Mark your answers **on the separate answer sheet**.

Tea at Ardmore

To reach Ardmore and take tea with Rebecca Ridgway you must make an expedition; not, perhaps an expedition in the Ridgway class, involving months of painstaking planning, physical training, mental preparation; not, when it's underway, the same degree of discomfort or edge of danger, but a prolonged exercise in transport arrangements in order to reach her crofthouse on a roadless peninsula near Cape Wrath, in the north-west corner of Scotland.

Rebecca does have neighbours; most importantly her parents, John and Marie-Christine Ridgway and one or two other self-sufficient solitaries who have settled in the remains of the crofting community of Ardmore. The Ridgways' extended crofthouse is not only the nerve-centre of the John Ridgway Adventure School, but the living heart of a community whose isolation is intensified by every storm from the Atlantic.

I walk along the peninsula towards the white house above the lake. Although Rebecca now lives in the cottage next door, she is waiting with Marie-Christine in the family kitchen, mugs on the table and kettle on the boil. Mother and daughter share the same slight figures and delicate good looks, but their grace disguises a toughness built up on daily five-mile runs and early morning swims in the freezing waters of the lake.

'Dad's out there somewhere,' says Rebecca, waving a hand at the mountain view, 'with some of his students.' Each year, many of the same people turn up for the Adventure School's women's course of hillwalking and sailing. Ardmore welcomes are always warm, and there is news to exchange; much has happened to the Ridgways since we last met – not least Rebecca's voyage in a canoe round tempestuous Cape Horn. And now, after twenty-five seasons, the family are to close the school for a time and sail away (not exactly round the world, which John and Marie-Christine have already done when they raced their boat *English Rose VII,* or merely across the Atlantic, which John rowed with Chay Blyth in 1966), but round the land mass of South America. All three will make the eighteen-month voyage.

'Dad's been trying to persuade us to do this trip for years, although Mum always swore she'd never sail with him again. He makes everything so stressful and we all get dreadfully seasick. But we need a break from the school.'

The timing, from Rebecca's point of view, couldn't be more perfect. Since she canoed round the Horn and wrote the book which describes that singular adventure she feels 'the pressure is off'. For years she has been set the example of high-achieving parents – the driven, demanding ex-soldier and his deceptively fragile-looking wife, 'who is tougher than any of us, who works harder than any of us, who is my main inspiration' – and now feels she has done the 'something amazing' that was expected of her. 'Cape Horn was Mum's suggestion, although it's Dad who usually sets the toughest challenges.' Marie-Christine says her bright idea subsequently gave her more than a few sleepless nights.

'I suppose I've always been trying to prove something to Dad,' continues Rebecca, 'Not so much seek his approval as get some recognition. When I was younger I was a bit scared of this figure who marched about barking orders. But since we've travelled together – even sharing tents, for heaven's sake – I feel I've got to know him better.'

She is more relaxed about the future than she's ever been, less anxious about 'finding some kind of sensible qualification, like physiotherapy' to back up all the skills acquired on land and water, as shepherd, sailor, outdoor pursuits instructor and now writer fighting with a lap-top computer in the South Atlantic to send articles to the *Daily Telegraph*.

95

8 It is a challenge to take tea with Rebecca Ridgway because
A she lives in a dangerous spot.
B it is difficult to persuade her to meet people.
C she expects her guests to be very fit.
D it is difficult to get to her home.

9 What does 'it' in line 6 refer to?
A planning
B tea
C an exercise
D an expedition

10 What are we told about Rebecca's home?
A It is part of a settlement which used to be bigger.
B It is the only house in the area.
C It is shared with her parents.
D It has been damaged in a storm.

11 What has Rebecca gained from the expedition round Cape Horn?
A She has satisfied her parents' ambitions for her.
B She has done something which her father was unable to achieve.
C She has shown that she is stronger than her parents.
D She has found out that she is a good writer.

12 What is her relationship with her father like?
A She wishes he were less strict.
B She wants him to notice her.
C She is still frightened of him.
D She wishes he were more like her mother.

13 What do we learn about Marie-Christine?
A She is not as fit as she used to be.
B She has never been very keen on sailing.
C She is stronger than she looks.
D She has always expected too much of her daughter.

14 How does Rebecca feel about the future?
A She would like to have a change.
B She is happy with the way things are going.
C She wants to qualify as a physiotherapist.
D She would like to have more time to write.

PART 3

*You are going to read a report of an interview with a film star. Eight sentences have been removed from the interview. Choose from the sentences (**A–I**) the one which fits each gap (**15–21**). There is one extra sentence which you do not need to use. There is an example at the beginning (**0**).*
Mark your answers **on the separate answer sheet**.

Having a wonderful time

Judy Sloane meets Hollywood star **Douglas Fairbanks Junior**, son of the famous actor in silent movies. Fairbanks Junior has made an extremely successful career of his own.

Being brought up in a show business family, did you want to be an actor?

Well, it wasn't a show business family. [0] [*I*] I couldn't help but be aware of it to a certain extent, because people would come around but the talk was very seldom shop-talk.

During your long and successful career you've certainly made the name Fairbanks your own, but when you were starting out was it a nuisance to you to be named after your father?

I think it probably was. It was a mixture in a way. It was useful in having the door open to get interviews, and to be allowed in to talk to the boss. [15]

Were you and your father close?

Not at first. We were just shy of each other. I think we were always fond of each other. [16] It wasn't until I was in my late twenties that we got to know each other very well.

Was your father a big influence in your life?

Not really, except I certainly took notice of his wonderful good nature with people. [17] It was a natural friendliness, and I admired that and I probably wanted to give that same impression when I was young.

Out of all your father's films, do you have a favourite one?

I think my very favourite one is 'Thief Of Baghdad'. It was one of the finest films ever made by anybody. [18] He was the guide and more or less the creator.

When did you know that you wanted to become an actor yourself?

When my mother and I were living abroad because it was cheaper, and mother's family had run out of money and we didn't know quite what to do, and somebody offered me a job! **19** [ ] It was a job at Paramount Pictures to play in a film called 'Stephen Steps Out' for which I got $1,000 a week for two weeks.

Your role as Rupert of Hentzau in 'The Prisoner Of Zenda' was one of your greatest.

It was a wonderful, wonderful part. **20** [ ] Then I had this offer to come back and do 'Prisoner Of Zenda'. I thought I'd better stick with this new company I'd started. My father was around and he said, 'Don't be a fool, you've got to go back, give up everything and play in "The Prisoner Of Zenda". It's the best part ever written'. And that decided me so I said, 'Yes, I will!'

Do you like the films they're making today?

The films themselves are all right. **21** [ ] There are still some very fine films that are being made, but some of them are of questionable taste and I blame the public. Being a business and an industry, producers produce what people buy. If the public don't like it, they won't go, and the films will stop being produced.

A The same talents are there, it's the public that has changed.

B He was always very nice to everybody he talked to, and he didn't have to pretend.

C That's when I decided!

D It should have been better.

E But it didn't make the jobs any easier, in fact it probably made them harder, because they expected more than I was able to deliver at a young age.

F We didn't quite know how to show it.

G I think it's a great work of art, and although a lot of people are credited with having a hand in it, everybody did more or less as my father wanted.

H In fact I didn't know whether to accept it or not, because I'd been struggling for years to have my own company in Europe and I was just getting started on that.

I Only my father was in the business, and it wasn't brought home.

PART 4

You are going to read an article about a family trying a vegetarian diet. For questions 22–35, choose from the people in the box (A–E). Some of the people may be chosen more than once. When more than one answer is required, these may be given in any order.
There is an example at the beginning (0).
Mark your answers on the separate answer sheet.

A Sue	**B** Michael	**C** Jo	**D** Mary	**E** Robin

Which person:

changed one of the recipes?	**0**	*A*		
doesn't miss meat at all?	**22**		**23**	
prefers dishes which are not too spicy?	**24**			
was keenest to try the diet?	**25**			
likes dishes to have plenty of taste?	**26**			
finds the new diet allows less time for doing other things?	**27**			
misses some of the foods the family no longer eats?	**28**		**29**	
has found the experience very rewarding in terms of ideas?	**30**			
can't eat too much vegetarian food?	**31**			

already knew quite a lot about healthy eating?

32	

likes to eat meat sometimes?

33		34	

will probably give up eating fish soon?

35	

TAKING THE
plunge

If you're thinking about the idea of turning vegetarian but are afraid it may be boring or too expensive, think again. Last October, we challenged a typical meat-eating family to go on a vegetarian diet for at least seven days.

GET SET

Sue Kent, 42, said 'I'm quite health conscious when it comes to food, so we'd already started to cut out red meat.' To start the week, and put everyone in the right frame of mind, Sue prepared a family favourite, vegetarian chilli. The rest of the week followed like a dream. 'The recipes all went down extremely well,' says Sue. 'The tomato and pasta soup was popular, as was the pasta with tomato and mozzarella sauce, although I've altered it, using a vegetarian blue cheese sauce because that's one of our favourites. I've carried on doing fish which most of us like.'

ALL CHANGE!

The Kents were so impressed by the flavours and variety of their new food regime that when the week ended they decided to continue on a largely vegetarian diet.

But making the change wasn't all plain sailing. 'The big drawback is all the preparation involved,' says Sue. 'It takes much longer than before because of all the chopping.'

So do they feel healthier for their new eating habits? 'It's hard to say, but I think on the whole we do,' says Sue. 'I certainly experiment more with my cooking and use many more herbs and spices than I used to. I'm trying out lots of unusual vegetables that I wouldn't have tried before, such as okra. Vegetarian food is so interesting – it's opened my eyes to a whole new world of cooking!'

What's the overall verdict? Here's what each member of the Kent family had to say.

MICHAEL, 46

'I must say I have been quite impressed by some of the recipes Sue has prepared,' says Michael. 'I love curries and other spicy foods, and we have plenty of those. I reckon vegetable curry is every bit as good as meat curry. The one thing I do miss is the chewing you do with meat, something substantial to get your teeth into. If I was out to dinner I don't think I would refuse a steak. I do miss roast lamb but on the whole I think it has been a great success.'

JO, 16

Jo was the main driving force behind the family trying our plan – and the biggest convert, becoming a strict vegetarian after taking up our challenge.

'Jo used to eat chicken, but she doesn't touch meat or fish at all now,' says Sue. 'She doesn't even miss sausages!'

MARY, 81

Michael's mother was the most hesitant about vegetarianism, but nevertheless she tried everything and liked many of the dishes. However, she did find that too much vegetarian food can affect her digestion.

'It's been quite interesting but I wouldn't like to think I was never going to eat meat again,' she says. 'I prefer simpler, plain foods like egg and cheese or fish to the more exotic foods like okra and peppers. I've never liked herbs and spices either, and I'm not much of a pasta fan.'

SUE, 42

'I'd quite happily never eat meat again, although I'd find it hard to go without fish.'

ROBIN, 2

Robin currently eats fish but he doesn't really care for it so Sue expects he'll be a total vegetarian before long. 'Apart from that, he's not a fussy eater – on a good day he'll eat anything,' says Sue. 'He loves pasta, and vegetable soup goes down well.'

PAPER 2 WRITING (1 hour 30 minutes)

PART 1

*You **must** answer this question.*

1   You are a student at the Swansea College of Higher Education and are the
    secretary of the History Society. You have invited someone called Mr
    Stephens to speak to the Society, but have just realised that you won't be
    able to meet his train which arrives at 4.45. Your diary, a notice about his visit,
    and a map are shown below.

    Look at the diary, the notice and the map. Then write a letter to Mr Stephens
    using all the relevant information. Apologise for not being able to meet the train,
    explain why and suggest how he should get to the college from the station.

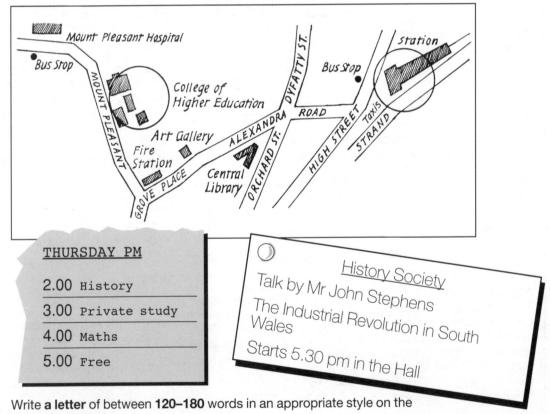

THURSDAY PM

2.00 History

3.00 Private study

4.00 Maths

5.00 Free

History Society
Talk by Mr John Stephens
The Industrial Revolution in South
Wales
Starts 5.30 pm in the Hall

Write **a letter** of between **120–180** words in an appropriate style on the
opposite page. Do not write any addresses.

PART 1

....
....
....
....
....
....
....
....
....
....
....
....
....
....
....
....
....
....
....
....
....
....
....
....
....
....
....
....
....
....
....

PART 2

*Write an answer to **one** of the questions **2–5** in this part. Write your answer in **120–180** words in an appropriate style on the opposite page, putting the question number in the box.*

2   Your penfriend in Britain asks the following question in his or her latest letter:

> I'd like to try preparing a traditional dish from your country. Can you tell me how to do it?

Briefly **describe a typical dish** in your country and give instructions on how to prepare and serve it.

3   A local English-language paper runs a readers' column called **My big mistake**. Write a **story** for the column, describing the circumstances and effects of your mistake, and explaining why it happened.

4   Your teacher has asked you to write about two photographs from your family album which are of particular importance to you. **Describe** what the pictures show and what memories they bring back for you.

5   **Background reading texts**

Answer **one** of the following two questions based on your reading of **one** of the set books (see p.2). Write the title of the book next to the question number box.

Either (a) Describe a moment which changes the course of the story and say why you think it is particularly important.

or (b) Choose one of the important relationships in the book and describe how it develops.

PART 2

Question	

....
....
....
....
....
....
....
....
....
....
....
....
....
....
....
....
....
....
....
....
....
....
....
....
....
....
....
....

PAPER 3   USE OF ENGLISH (1 hour 15 minutes)

PART 1

*For questions **1–15**, read the text below and decide which answer **A, B, C** or **D**
best fits each space. There is an example at the beginning (**0**).
Mark your answers **on the separate answer sheet**.*

Example:
0   A descends   **B** falls   **C** drops   **D** jumps

0	A	B	C	D
	▬	▢	▢	▢

ANGER ON THE ROADS

The anger that **(0)** .... on people when they get behind the steering wheel of a car
used to be **(1)** .... as a joke. But the laughter is getting noticeably quieter **(2)** .... that
the problem has become increasingly widespread.

(3) .... in a traffic jam, with family cars inching their **(4)** .... past, the driver of a fast
sports car begins to lose his temper. **(5)** .... the capabilities of his car, there is
nothing he can do. The **(6)** .... is anger.

Many people live in **(7)** .... of losing control. This is true of many situations but
driving is a good example. People think that the car might not start, it might break
(8) .... , or someone might run into it. Before anything even happens, people have
worked themselves up into a **(9)** .... of anxiety. And when something does happen,
they're **(10)** .... to explode. In fact, it's their very anxiety about losing control that
(11) .... them lose control.

This isn't to **(12)** .... that all offenders have psychological problems or drive
powerful sports cars. In fact, most of them are **(13)** .... ordinary human beings who
have no history of violence. There is **(14)** .... something deep in our nature that
(15) .... when we start up a car engine.

1 **A** found   **B** thought   **C** treated   **D** intended

2 **A** once   **B** even   **C** since   **D** now

3 **A** Set   **B** Stuck   **C** Held   **D** Fixed

4 **A** path   **B** way   **C** course   **D** route

5 **A** However   **B** Besides   **C** Although   **D** Despite

6 **A** outcome   **B** event   **C** issue   **D** effect

7 **A** worry   **B** fright   **C** fear   **D** concern

8 **A** up   **B** down   **C** out   **D** off

9 **A** state   **B** condition   **C** feeling   **D** case

10 **A** good   **B** prepared   **C** near   **D** ready

11 **A** causes   **B** leads   **C** makes   **D** forces

12 **A** inform   **B** say   **C** tell   **D** announce

13 **A** purely   **B** fully   **C** exactly   **D** perfectly

14 **A** openly   **B** directly   **C** clearly   **D** frankly

15 **A** excites   **B** awakens   **C** disturbs   **D** upsets

PART 2

*For questions **16–30**, read the text below and think of the word which best fits each space. Use only **one** word in each space. There is an example at the beginning (**0**).*
*Write your word **on the separate answer sheet**.*

Example: | 0 | *to* | 0 — — |

MISSION TO MARS

The Americans are keen to win the race **(0)** .... send human beings to Mars. In 1992, the new boss of NASA*, Dan Goldin, called on the American people to be the first to send explorers to **(16)** .... planet in the solar system. He reminded them **(17)** .... the symbolic gift carried to the moon and back by the Apollo 11 mission. It bears **(18)** .... message intended for the crew of the first spaceship to visit Mars. Goldin thinks **(19)** .... is time to begin the preparations **(20)** .... this historic journey. His speech echoed the words of the President, **(21)** ... promised that in 2019, 50 years after Neil Armstrong **(22)** .... the first man to set foot on the Moon, the first astronaut **(23)** .... stand on Mars.

(24) .... the end of the twentieth century, various unmanned spaceships will **(25)** .... thoroughly investigated the surface of the planet. But, however clever a robot **(26)** .... be, it cannot match the type of information **(27)** .... can be gained from direct human experience. The first geologist on the moon, Harrison Schmitt, was **(28)** .... of interpreting the story of the landscape on the spot. **(29)** .... humans walk on the red deserts of Mars, we will not be able to determine the history of this frozen world **(30)** .... any detail.

* The North American Space Agency

PART 3

*For questions **31–40**, complete the second sentence so that it has a similar meaning to the first sentence, using the word given. **Do not change the word given**. You must use between two and five words, including the word given. There is an example at the beginning (**0**).*
*Write **only** the missing words **on the separate answer sheet**.*

Example:

0 I last saw him at my 21st birthday party.
   since

   I .... my 21st birthday party.

The gap can be filled by the words 'haven't seen him since' so you write:

0	*haven't seen him since*	0	0 1 2

---

31 'Why don't you wait by the phone box, Brenda?' said Leslie.
   Brenda

   Leslie suggested .... by the phone box.

32 Although he overslept, Clive wasn't late for work.
   up

   Despite .... on time, Clive wasn't late for work.

33 I haven't eaten food like this before.
   time

   This is the .... this sort of food.

34 After a long chase, the police finally succeeded in arresting the thief.
   to

   After a long chase, the police finally .... the thief.

35 Diane was supposed to write to her parents last week.
   ought

   Diane .... to her parents last week.

36 His handwriting is so small I can hardly read it.
such

He .... I can hardly read it.

37 Somebody has to pick the visitors up from the airport.
up

The visitors .... from the airport.

38 I wish I hadn't told him what we were planning to do this evening.
regret

I .... for this evening.

39 Everyone was surprised to see Geoff leave the party early.
surprise

To .... the party early.

40 All the witnesses said the accident was my fault.
blame

All the witnesses said that .... the accident.

For questions **41–55**, read the text below and look carefully at each line. Some of the lines are correct, and some have a word which should not be there. If a line is correct, put a tick (✓) by the number **on the separate answer sheet**. If a line has a word which should **not** be there, write the word **on the separate answer sheet**. There are two examples at the beginning (**0** and **00**).

Examples:

0	*to*	0
00	✓	0

A MUCH-IMPROVED JOURNEY

0	Shortly after reaching to Weymouth on the south coast of England
00	on holiday, we caught sight of a small white dot on the horizon,
41	moving at an amazing speed. Surely it couldn't be a ship going so
42	fast? We thought it might still be a trick of the light, but as the shape
43	came closer, it was clear so that we had not been mistaken: it was
44	indeed some sort of a ship and it was travelling very much faster
45	than a normal boat could ever have done in similar conditions.
46	It turned out as to be the new high-speed ferry to the Channel
47	Islands, which could reach Guernsey in just over the two hours. This
48	seemed incredible since the last time when we had visited the island,
49	it had taken us for five hours to get there, but now, with this faster
50	service, a day trip it was clearly a real possibility and we decided to
51	buy tickets for the next day. It also meant getting to the harbour by six
52	o'clock but it was certainly worth making the effort to get up early.
53	The weather was fine and the ferry lived well up to its claims for a
54	comfortable crossing. By half past nine we were relaxing ourselves in
55	a Guernsey café, enjoying a leisurely breakfast and looking out across
	the sea.

PART 5

*For questions **56–65**, read the text below. Use the word given in capitals at the end of each line to form a word that fits in the space in the same line. There is an example at the beginning (**0**). Write your word **on the separate answer sheet**.*

Example:	0	*marvellous*	0 __ __

THE ABC OF COOKING

It's a **(0)** .... idea for children to do some cooking at an early   **MARVEL**
age. Generally **(56)** .... , most children can't wait to help in the   **SPEAK**
kitchen and love getting involved in the **(57)** .... of their meals.   **PREPARE**
They should be **(58)** .... to do so, and care should be taken to   **COURAGE**
(59) .... they enjoy the experience. It is important to show them   **SURE**
how to do things **(60)** .... but they shouldn't be criticised too much.   **CORRECT**
Although the finished result may not be quite to your **(61)** .... , the   **LIKE**
young cook will undoubtedly find it quite the **(62)** .... food he or   **TASTY**
she has ever eaten.

Kitchens can, of course, be **(63)** .... places and so the absolute   **DANGER**
(64) .... of keeping an eye on children at all times cannot be   **IMPORTANT**
emphasised too **(65)** .... . Sharp knives, for example, should be   **HEAVY**
avoided until children are old enough to handle them safely.

PAPER 4   LISTENING (approximately 40 minutes)

PART 1

You will hear people talking in eight different situations.
*For questions **1–8**, choose the best answer **A, B** or **C**.*

1   These women are talking about a colleague.
What do they feel about his behaviour?

A   It was typical of him.

B   It had improved.

C   It reminded them of someone else.

1

2   This man is talking about a sports event.
What happened to his team?

A   They won.

B   They did better than he'd hoped.

C   They were very unlucky.

2

3   Listen to this man telephoning someone about his washing machine.
Who is he talking to?

A   an engineer

B   a friend

C   the shop he bought it from

3

4   You switch on the radio and hear this report.
Where is it coming from?

A   a market

B   a concert hall

C   a racetrack

4

5 You hear this man talking about his bad back.
How did he injure it?

  A in a road accident

  B by lifting something

  C in a fight

5

6 You overhear these people talking about a book.
What sort of book is it?

  A a guidebook

  B a history book

  C a novel

6

7 Listen to this woman who has just arrived at a meeting.
Why is she late?

  A The weather was bad.

  B There was a traffic jam.

  C She crashed her car.

7

8 At the sports club you hear these people discussing an exercise.
What is its purpose?

  A to help you lose weight

  B to make you relax

  C to strengthen the stomach muscles

8

PART 2

You will hear part of a radio programme about holidays.
For questions 9–18, complete the grid.

	Eastingham	Brant	Faresey
Main attraction	9	13	16
Size	10	14	
Best transport to get there	11	15	17
Best time of year	12		18

PART 3

You will hear five people talking about clothes.
*For questions **19–23**, choose from the list **A–F** what each speaker is talking about.*
Use the letters only once. There is one extra letter which you do not need to use.

A   a hat

B   a shirt

C   an overcoat

D   a suit

E   a sock

F   a boot

Speaker 1		**19**
Speaker 2		**20**
Speaker 3		**21**
Speaker 4		**22**
Speaker 5		**23**

PART 4

You will hear two friends discussing evening study courses.
*For questions **24–30**, decide which course each statement refers to.*
Mark   **A** *for Art*
      or   **C** *for Computers*
      or   **S** *for Spanish*

24   You must book a place on this course.

	24

25   Polly already knows this subject.

	25

26   This course is taught by a qualified teacher.

	26

27   There's an extra charge for this course.

	27

28   This course lasts for two terms.

	28

29   Students work hard on this course.

	29

30   Polly would do this course if she had time.

	30

PAPER 5   SPEAKING (approximately 15 minutes)

Part 1

You tell the examiner about yourself. The examiner may ask you questions such as: Where are you from? How do you usually spend your free time? What are your plans for the future? Your partner does the same.

Part 2

The examiner gives you two pictures to look at and asks you to talk about them for about a minute. Your partner does the same with two different pictures.

Part 3

The examiner gives you a photograph or drawing to look at with your partner. You are asked to solve a problem or come to a decision about something in the picture. For example, you might be asked to decide the best way to use some rooms in a language school. You discuss the problem together.

Part 4

You are asked more questions connected with your discussion in Part 3. For example, you might be asked to talk about the best ways of studying.

Keys and Tapescripts

Test 1 Key

Paper 1 Reading

Part 1

1 C   2 F   3 H   4 A   5 G   6 E   7 B

Part 2

8 B   9 D   10 A   11 B   12 D   13 B   14 A   15 C

Part 3

16 B   17 D   18 G   19 E   20 A   21 C

Part 4

22 and 23 A/C   24 B   25 C   26 F   **27 and 28** D/H   29 D
30 G   31 C   32 A   **33 and 34** E/G   35 H
(Where there are two possible answers, these are interchangeable.)

Paper 2 Writing

Part 1

Plan

> letter to Mr Lawrence
> seen advert – thinking of attending
> pls send info & prices
>
> questions:
> * students   – how many?
>   – ages?
> * sports programme – includes?
> * amenities (eg? pool, cinema)
> * staff = qualified teachers?
> +
> music – family + piano to practise?
>
> look forward reply

Model answer

> Dear Mr Lawrence,
>
> I have seen your advertisement for summer language courses and I am thinking of attending one for two or three weeks. Could you please send me more information and details of prices?
>
> I would particularly like to know how many students attend the school, their ages and how many students there are in a class. Also, can you explain what is included in the sports programme and what amenities there are near the school? For example, is there a cinema or swimming-pool in Little Bonnington? Could you tell me something about your staff? Are they all qualified teachers?
>
> Lastly, as I am a music student, I would very much like to stay with a family who have a piano that I can practise on. Do you think it would be possible to arrange this?
>
> I look forward to receiving your reply.
>
> Yours sincerely,
>
> Daniel Rovetta

(147 words)

Part 2 Question 2

Plan

<u>article</u>

Introduction
Parents complain – they are talking about career
Choosing career very difficult – affects all life

Explanation
- career – want interest & money
    so, mistake = regret for ever
    therefore, hesitate

- ideal company
    eg   not harm environment
        feel useful in society
    hard to find

Conclusion
– know what we want, but can we get it?

Model answer

Many parents complain about their children because they do not seem to know what they want from life. When they say this, it is usually because they want their children to choose a career. Choosing a career is difficult and it affects your whole life.

Most young people want a job which is both interesting and well-paid. They know that if they choose badly when they are young, they may regret their mistake for ever. Therefore, they hesitate about their career.

Young people also have ideals and they want a job which matches these. For example, they may want to avoid working for a company which harms the environment. They may want to feel useful in society. Jobs like this can be hard to find.

My conclusion is that young people do know what they want from life. Unfortunately, they are not so sure whether they can get it!

(150 words)

Part 2 Question 3

Plan

<u>story</u>

Alex – our school – I was 8
He = old-fashioned clothes, hair, manners (grandmother)
Teased – not me

before school – football game – older boy pushed me –
tore jeans – late – no trouble

teacher after class – question me – Alex explained for me
thank Alex –

Model answer

When I was eight, Alex came to our school. He lived with his grandmother. His clothes and hairstyle were old-fashioned and so were his manners. Some of the children teased him about these things, but I didn't, because I felt sorry for him.

One day a group of us had a game of football on the way to school. One of the older boys pushed me and I fell over and tore my jeans very badly. I had to go home to change. I arrived very late for school. I expected to get into trouble about it, but nothing happened.

After class, the teacher asked me who had pushed me. Of course I answered 'I can't say.' Then I asked how he knew about it. He said 'Alex told me what happened, but he didn't say who pushed you.' Then he told me to be more careful in future.

That afternoon I walked home with Alex and thanked him for what he had done. No matter what people said about Alex, I knew he was a true friend.

(179 words)

Part 2 Question 4

Plan

REPORT

Pool
Opening times
How to get there – bus, bicycle

<u>Good</u> – clean, well run
            staff
            drinks machine

<u>Bad</u> – changing rooms crowded
            queue for showers

<u>Café</u> – times
            food, prices
            outside tables

Recommend for after school

Model answer

<u>Griffon Swimming-pool (outdoor heated pool and café)</u>
Entrance £2
Open   7 am – 7 pm Monday – Saturday
          8 am – 7 pm Sunday

<u>How to get there from our school:</u>
        By bus – Number 55 bus runs from outside the school every 15 minutes. Ask for Griffon Pool. Costs 50 pence. Takes 15 minutes.

        By bicycle – Go straight into town, pass City Hall, turn right into Griffon Place. Takes about 20 minutes.

This is a good, medium-sized pool. It's clean and well run. The staff are friendly and helpful. There is a cold drinks machine (50 pence coins) outside the changing rooms. The changing rooms are rather crowded at busy times and you often have to queue for a shower.

There is also a small café which is open from 10.30 am to 7 pm. It has sandwiches, drinks and salads. The prices are reasonable and the food is fresh. Some of the tables are outside so you can watch people swimming while you eat.

I recommend this as a pleasant place to relax with your classmates after school.

(176 words)

Paper 3 Use of English

Award one mark for each correct answer, except in Part 3, where two marks are available, divided up as shown, for each answer.

Correct spelling is essential throughout. Ignore omission or abuse of capital letters. No half marks.

Part 1

1 B   2 A   3 C   4 D   5 A   6 D   7 D   8 B
9 C   10 A   11 D   12 C   13 B   14 A   15 A

Part 2

16 where   17 how   18 anyone/anybody   19 tried/attempted/threatened
20 after   21 no   22 a/per/each/every   23 The   24 whose
25 yet/but/(al)though   26 of   27 as   28 If/Provided/Providing
29 to   30 will/can

Part 3

31 accused Frank of (1) breaking/having broken (1)
32 must have/get (1) my car (1)
33 wishes she (1) had bought (1)
34 if you (1) hadn't/had not helped (1) OR but for/without you/your (1) helping (1)
35 in case (1) I ran (1)
36 have fallen (1) through (1)
37 wasn't/was not (1) fresh enough (1)
38 may have (1) gone (1)
39 is/'s impossible (1) for me to (1)
40 was (1) being watched (1)

Part 4

41 much   42 until   43 ✓   44 it   45 myself   46 one
47 ✓   48 ✓   49 out   50 to   51 ✓   52 with   53 so
54 all   55 for

Part 5

56 life   57 noticing   58 originally   59 convenience   60 sale
61 widened   62 shorter   63 underground   64 likelihood
65 freedom

Paper 4 Listening

Part 1

1 B 2 C 3 B 4 A 5 B 6 A 7 B 8 A

Part 2

9 useful for future/helpful for career/wants to be a nurse *etc.*
10 farmhouse 11 road 12 lifts 13 (taking round) evening drinks
14 money/costs *etc.* 15 grateful (for extras) 16 her son-in-law
17 (an) equal/(just) the same (as them) 18 organise (a) concert

Part 3

19 B 20 A 21 C 22 F 23 E

Part 4

24 T 25 T 26 T 27 F 28 T 29 F 30 F

Tapescript *First Certificate Practice Test One. Paper Four. Listening. Hello, I'm going to give you the instructions for this test. I'll introduce each part of the test and give you time to look at the questions. At the start of each piece, you'll hear this sound:*

tone

You'll hear each piece twice.

Remember, while you're listening, write your answers on the question paper. You'll have time at the end of the test to copy your answers onto the separate answer sheet.
The tape will now be stopped. Please ask any questions now, because you must not speak during the test.

[pause]

PART 1 *Now, open your question paper and look at Part One.*
You'll hear people talking in eight different situations. For questions 1 to 8, choose the best answer, A, B or C.

Question 1 *One*
You are visiting a museum when you hear this man addressing a group of people. Who is he?
A a security guard
B a tourist guide
C a museum guide

[pause]

tone

Tourist guide: O.K. everyone, uh, before we go into the next room I'd like to warn you not to try and

143

touch any of the wall-hangings or furniture. As you will see they're very beautiful, with very delicate finishes. The museum is very strict about this and they will ask you to leave if they think you're not taking the rule seriously. I actually had someone told to leave when I brought a group here last year because he accidentally brushed against something. Um?

[pause]

tone

[The recording is repeated.]

[pause]

Question 2   *Two*
You're in a restaurant when you overhear one of the waiters talking. Who is he talking about?
A a colleague
B the manager
C a customer

[pause]

tone

Waiter: Well, I said, I don't stand for that sort of thing from anyone. I don't care whether they've been coming here since before I was born, they've no right to speak to anyone like that. I'm doing my job and it's my job to serve her a meal, not run up and down the road with messages. She's going to complain about me she said. Well, I'm going to complain about her!

[pause]

tone

[The recording is repeated.]

[pause]

Question 3   *Three*
You're waiting in a hospital corridor when you hear this woman talking. What does she say about her doctor?
A He's made a mistake.
B He's been unhelpful.
C He's been untruthful.

[pause]

tone

Woman: To be honest I thought at first he'd got my notes mixed up with someone else. We didn't seem to be talking about the same illness. He kept going on about how it's not uncommon for these side-effects to occur. And I thought, that's all very well for you to say, but I'm the only case I know, and I asked what he was going to do now. Well, he just sort of smiled, and said something about 'weighing discomfort against disease', really pompous! And that was it as far as he was concerned.

[pause]

tone

[The recording is repeated.]

[pause]

Question 4

Four
You are out shopping when you hear a shop assistant talking to a customer.
What is she refusing to do?
A give him some money
B change a faulty item
C repair something

[pause]

tone

Shop assistant:	Unfortunately, it's just not possible for me to do that. I don't have the authority, you see.
Man:	But, but, it's faulty. I know my rights.
Shop assistant:	But I can't tell if there's really anything wrong with it, just looking at it, so the best I can do is give you a credit note as if you'd changed your mind about wanting it. Then you can choose goods to the same value, well, either now or at a later date. Because we don't give cash refunds unless there's something actually wrong with the item. Otherwise, I can have it sent back for checking, but I still can't pay anything out till we've had confirmation of a fault.

[pause]

tone

[The recording is repeated.]

[pause]

Question 5

Five
Listen to this woman introducing the next speaker at a conference. Why has she been asked to introduce him?
A He is an old friend.
B He is a former student of hers.
C He is a colleague.

[pause]

tone

Conference chair:	Now, it gives me the greatest pleasure to introduce our keynote speaker. I take no small pride in having had even a minor role in the development of one of the most forward-thinking workers in his field. We shared many fascinating discussions as he raced through my course, too many years ago now. I can hardly claim to have taught, merely to have helped along the way, although he has been kind enough to say he learnt from me! Anyway, I'm very honoured to present to you ….

[pause]

tone

[The recording is repeated.]

[pause]

Question 6   *Six*
You are staying in a farmhouse when you hear your host on the telephone.
Who is he talking to?
A a supplier
B a customer
C an employee

[pause]

tone

Farmer: No, no, I'm sorry, I simply can't accept that. I'm running a business here, too, and I can't just turn round and tell my customers that, well, sorry, no vegetables this week, I haven't had time to pick them! I've got fields here waiting to be planted out. You've been telling me for a week you'd have the fertiliser in stock tomorrow. I need it on that field today. If you can't get it here I'll have to find someone else who can.

[pause]

tone

[The recording is repeated.]

[pause]

Question 7   *Seven*
You hear this critic talking on the radio. What is she recommending?
A a film
B a book
C an exhibition

[pause]

tone

Critic: I was really pleased to be asked to review this, because I was enormously curious to see whether Delaney could handle the change of medium, whether he could colour in the bits between the dialogue, so to speak. In fact I think he's done very well, and there's no sign of that horrid 'book of the film' feel that you sometimes get from people who are crossing over from script-writing to the novel. The characters are very finely drawn and right from the first chapter the plot is cleverly worked. I have some little doubts about …

[pause]

tone

[The recording is repeated.]

[pause]

Question 8   *Eight*
You are walking up the street when you hear this man talking to a woman at
her front door. What does he want to do?
A interview her
B help her
C advise her

[pause]

tone

Reporter: I won't keep you more than a few minutes, and I'm sure if you think about it, you'll realise that talking to someone like me will be a lot better than leaving people to make everything up. Because I can assure you, they will make it up, if you don't get your story out first, so why not just give me your side of things now?

[pause]

tone

[The recording is repeated.]

[pause]

That's the end of Part One.
Now turn to Part Two.

PART 2   *You will hear a student called Bill talking about his holiday job. For*
questions 9 to 18, complete the notes which summarise what he says. You
will need to write a word or a short phrase. You now have forty-five seconds
in which to look at Part Two.

[pause]

tone

Bill: Yeah, over last summer I did this job in an old people's home. I'd been looking for work and I said I wanted something which might be useful, because I want to train as a nurse when I finish school, so they said what about a care assistant, and I said, sure. So, anyway, I went along and it's in this old house, it was a farmhouse, but the farm's all gone, now the town's got bigger, and it's just got a bit of a garden round it. It's got a lawn and flowerbeds at the back, but the front is quite near the road. I was surprised but the old people like it they say, because they can watch what's going on a bit. You know, some places, they're very pretty, but so quiet and they feel cut off. It's quite a nice building, with lots of the old woodwork and so on, just they've put in a couple of lifts for obvious reasons, because they've got some quite frail people among the residents.

   I really liked the work, which was a relief, and I got on pretty well with most of the residents. Some of them were a good laugh. They like talking about when they were younger. The best part of my work was when I'd take round their evening drinks, I wouldn't be having to rush off, and I could take time to listen. I suppose they'd told all their stories before but I hadn't heard them, so I was a good audience.

   I didn't see much of Mrs Stone, that's the owner, but she seemed all right. She's got two or three of these places, and I think she's always concerned about whether she's going to lose money. But I don't think she's mean. She just can't afford not to be businesslike about it, or they'd go bust. The residents mostly seemed to like her, anyway. They were nice, most of them, one or two of the old girls could be a bit snappy, but I think that was their arthritis, and the old boys were all ever so grateful if you had time to do them any little extras. The only really tricky one was this old girl who thought I was her son-in-law, because of my hair being the same colour, and she didn't get on with her son-in-law, so she didn't get on with me. But I survived, anyway. The rest of the staff did what they could. It was really good, being treated just the same, like an equal, by very experienced people. It made me value my own work and try to do it as well as them. It was a really useful experience, and I learnt a lot. I'm going back there next month, because I'm organising a concert for them. They're looking forward to it. And what I wanted to ask, was whether anyone …

[pause]

tone

Now you'll hear Part Two again.

[The recording is repeated.]

[pause]

That's the end of Part Two.
Now turn to Part Three.

PART 3   *You will hear five different women talking about parties.*
For questions 19 to 23, choose from the list A to F what they describe. Use the letters only once. There is one extra letter which you do not need to use. You now have 30 seconds in which to look at Part Three.

[pause]

tone

First woman: I must admit that I was extremely reluctant. You know I don't go out much these days, I don't see many people and I tend to think that anything with more than a handful of people will be noisy and exhausting. But it was really pleasant. There was masses of room, lovely things to eat and drink, and when I discovered it was gone midnight I was amazed. The time had flown and I hadn't noticed.

[pause]

Second woman: Well, they said, Come on, you know how people do, so I went, I didn't want them to think I was being an old misery. After all, I don't often see them since we left college. But, I swear, that's the last time I let them drag me anywhere. I don't think they thought it was much fun either, though they wouldn't admit it of course, but I haven't been so bored for years. I should've stayed at home watching the rubbish on telly!

[pause]

Third woman: So anyway, they all decided they'd come too. And I said, 'But were you invited?' And they said, well, I don't know, they sort of implied they were. So I turned up with them and the girl who was giving the party, you don't know her, she's very nice, anyway she came to the door, and said 'Hello' to me and sort of looked at the others and then looked at me and I realised she thought I was taking advantage, and I went all hot and cold. Anyway we went in and I could see her looking at me from time to time, and I thought, well she won't ask me again, and I was longing to explain but I never had a chance. It was horrible. I'll never forgive them.

[pause]

Fourth woman: We all arrived and my friends went off to find drinks and things and I was just standing there feeling shy as usual and thinking, 'Why did I come?' And I saw this girl watching me, and I thought she'd noticed something wrong, so I was sort of checking myself in a mirror, trying not to look as if I was, then she came up and asked if I was Suzanne, and I said I was, and then she started on about my work. She knew all about it and said a lot of flattering things, in a very nice way. I enjoyed meeting her, she really made the evening for me. I wish I'd remembered to find out where she lived.

[pause]

Fifth woman: It was nearly a disaster. I mean, I wouldn't have missed the opportunity to meet him, but I'd had no idea it'd be swarming with children. And we were outdoors most of the time, so of course I was freezing, because I'd only got a shawl over my dress, trying to look smart. I needn't have bothered of course. Anyway, I, I did enjoy talking to him, although it wasn't for long enough really, and the food was wonderful. But, um, I think I'll swallow my pride and phone and check another time!

[pause]

tone

Now you'll hear Part Three again.

[The recording is repeated.]

[pause]

That's the end of Part Three.
Now turn to Part Four.

PART 4 *You will hear a conversation between two teenagers, Nick and Sandra. Decide whether statements 24 to 30 are true or false and mark your answers T for True or F for False. You now have forty-five seconds in which to look at Part Four.*

[pause]

tone

Nick: Hi, Sandra, where've you been?
Sandra: Oh, am I late? Sorry. I had to do some tidying up before I came out.
Nick: Yeah, I know. I hate getting home and finding I've still got to wash up from breakfast.
Sandra: It's not me that minds. It's my mother. She treats me like I was twelve or something. You've no idea how lucky you are to have your own place.
Nick: Well, you'd have to do it eventually, wouldn't you?
Sandra: I don't see why. It's my room, she doesn't have to come poking in there and telling me what to do.
Nick: Well, I guess if you don't mind the mess and it's just your room, then I suppose she should let you. Personally, I like to be able to find things in a hurry.

Sandra:	I can find things when I want to. What really gets me is she makes me do all sorts of stupid chores every Saturday round the house.
Nick:	Well, she can't do them all.
Sandra:	She isn't going anywhere. She's got all weekend to do them.
Nick:	Oh, come on. Why should she do housework all weekend while you enjoy yourself?
Sandra:	She hasn't got exams next month. I haven't got time.
Nick:	I think you're being a bit unreasonable. You have time to come and meet me.
Sandra:	That's different.
Nick:	No, it isn't.
Sandra:	Whose side are you on, here?
Nick:	Look, perhaps I just have a better idea how much your Mum has to get through. When you're responsible for a place it makes a lot of difference.
Sandra:	Oh, don't be such a pain. Are you going to keep lecturing me all evening or are we going to see this band?
Nick:	Sure. Have you brought the tickets?
Sandra:	What tickets?
Nick:	I got them on Thursday and gave them to you to look after. Don't you remember? You put them in your jeans pocket.
Sandra:	You're teasing me. Oh no! Mum washed these jeans yesterday. I bet she never checked the pockets. Oh, I'll kill her!
Nick:	Well, have a look. Anyway, I don't see why she should check your pockets.
Sandra:	Okay, okay. Don't start that again. Oh no, wait a minute, this might be them. Do you think they're all right? They're a bit crumpled.
Nick:	Honestly! Next time I'd better look after them myself. I'm sure they'll be OK. Now, get a move on, or we won't get in after all this.

[pause]

tone

Now you'll hear Part Four again.

[The recording is repeated.]

[pause]

That is the end of Part Four.
There'll now be a pause of five minutes for you to copy your answers onto the separate answer sheet.
I'll remind you when there's one minute left, so that you're sure to finish in time.

[pause]

You have one more minute left.

[pause]

That's the end of the test. Please stop now. Your supervisor will now collect all the question papers and answer sheets.
Goodbye.

Test 2 Key

Paper 1 Reading

Part 1
1 C   2 H   3 D   4 A   5 G   6 F   7 B

Part 2
8 C   9 C   10 B   11 A   12 C   13 D   14 B   15 A

Part 3
16 G   17 A   18 C   19 E   20 D   21 B

Part 4
22 B   23 D   24 E   25 H   26 and 27 G/H   28 A
29 D   30 C   31 B   32 E   33 and 34 A/E   35 C
(Where there are two possible answers, these are interchangeable.)

Paper 2 Writing

Part 1 – Plan

---

letter to friend

why I'm writing

my experience compared to advert
- class size
- pay & travel expenses
- free time
- August easier

my advice

Paper 3 Use of English

Award one mark for each correct answer, except in Part 3, where two marks are available, divided up as shown, for each answer.

Correct spelling is essential throughout. Ignore omission or abuse of capital letters. No half marks.

Part 1

1 C   2 D   3 A   4 B   5 D   6 B   7 A   8 A
9 C   10 D   11 A   12 B   13 A   14 C   15 D

Part 2

16 as   17 how/what   18 it   19 into/to/through   20 or/and
21 since   22 by   23 the/those   24 of   25 been   26 In
27 are   28 this   29 which   30 fact

Part 3

31 whose coat (1) this (1) OR whose (1) this coat (1)
32 prevented her (1) (from) taking (1)
33 must not be (1) ridden (1) OR must be (1) pushed/carried/wheeled (1)
34 was amazed (1) to find (1)
35 don't need to/needn't/need not (1) book (1)
36 too high (1) for (any of) (1)
37 would/'d rather (1) you started (1)
38 they remembered (1) what (they had) (1)
39 hardly ever (1) loses her (1)
40 have/'ve run (1) out of (1)

Part 4

41 for   42 the   43 of   44 ✓   45 ✓   46 more   47 will
48 much   49 ✓   50 ever   51 only   52 ✓   53 a   54 at
55 it

Part 5

56 settlement   57 southern   58 earliest   59 uninhabited
60 surrounded   61 building   62 religious   63 successfully
64 development   65 central

Paper 4 Listening

Part 1

1 B   2 A   3 C   4 A   5 C   6 C   7 A   8 B

Part 2

9 (in the) suburbs   10 librarian   11 (about) once a week
12 should (stay) open later   13 too high/not cheap   14 need modernising
15 (more) showers   16 athletics   17 local business(es)   18 pensioners

Part 3

19 C   20 D   21 E   22 B   23 A

Part 4

24 T   25 F   26 F   27 T   28 T   29 F   30 F

Tapescript   *First Certificate Practice Test Two. Paper Four. Listening. Hello, I'm going to give you the instructions for this test. I'll introduce each part of the test and give you time to look at the questions. At the start of each piece, you'll hear this sound:*

tone

You'll hear each piece twice.
Remember, while you're listening, write your answers on the question paper. You'll have time at the end of the test to copy your answers onto the separate answer sheet.
The tape will now be stopped. Please ask any questions now, because you must not speak during the test.

[pause]

PART 1   *Now, open your question paper and look at Part One.*
You'll hear people talking in eight different situations. For questions 1 to 8, choose the best answer, A, B or C.

Question 1   One
You are walking round a market when you hear this woman talking to a customer. What is she doing?
A asking the customer's opinion
B offering a cheap sample
C explaining a price rise

[pause]

tone

Market trader: Look, I tell you what. You just take a couple home tonight, I'll knock off fifty pence, how's that? And try them – you'll love 'em, I promise you – and then tomorrow you can come and tell me if I'm not right. What d'you say to that, then? I can't say fairer than that, now can I?

[pause]

tone

[The recording is repeated.]

[pause]

Question 2   Two
You're in the doctor's waiting room when you overhear the nurse on the phone. Why didn't she send off the notes?
A She didn't know they were wanted.
B It isn't part of her job to do it.
C She didn't know which notes to send.

[pause]

tone

Nurse: No, I haven't received anything. ... Well, I do, normally, but even if our receptionist had, she'd have told me straight away. ... Of course I'll go and look the notes out now and send them off straight away. Now, what was the patient's name again?

[pause]

tone

[The recording is repeated.]

[pause]

Question 3 *Three*
You're in a gallery when you hear these women talking. What are they looking at?
A *a bowl*
B *a lamp*
C *a vase*

[pause]

tone

First woman: It's very lovely, isn't it?
Second woman: Well, I suppose so, but it's not really practical, is it? I mean, it's so tall and thin you'd be afraid of knocking it over. Or would you actually put flowers in it?
First woman: Oh, really! You'd put it somewhere where the light could shine through, just to look at it. You wouldn't want to use it. Not at that price!

[pause]

tone

[The recording is repeated.]

[pause]

Question 4 *Four*
You are visiting a large company and you hear two people talking. What are they discussing?
A *a personal computer*
B *a typewriter*
C *a CD player*

[pause]

tone

Woman: Look, we can put it here on the table.
Man: Yes, that'll leave the desk clear for papers and things. But, er, will the light be OK? You don't want it reflecting on the screen.
Woman: No, that's all right. I can turn it at an angle. Shall I go and get the disks and things?
Man: No, don't bother, I'll bring them up later.

[pause]

tone

[The recording is repeated.]

[pause]

Question 5   *Five*
Listen to this clerk at a station booking office. Which is the cheapest ticket?
A   a period return
B   an ordinary return
C   a Rover

[pause]

tone

Railway clerk: Well, you can either get a period return, if you're going to be away more than three nights, or you can get an ordinary return that leaves you free to come back any time, but of course it costs more, although it's cheaper than two singles, of course. Or you can get a Rover ticket, which allows unlimited travel within the region for up to seven days. That's cheaper than the period return, and you can go further, but of course not at rush hours.

[pause]

tone

[The recording is repeated.]

[pause]

Question 6   *Six*
These friends are talking about a film. Who will go to see it?
A   both of them
B   neither of them
C   the girl

[pause]

tone

Girl: I really think you ought to give it a chance. You aren't usually so narrow-minded.
Boy: I'm not. But Barry said his Dad really enjoyed it. We've got no tastes in common I ever heard about, so I know what it'll be like.
Girl: Well, I think you're silly. You'll be sorry when I tell you how funny it was.

[pause]

tone

[The recording is repeated.]

[pause]

Question 7   *Seven*
These people are talking about a colleague. What's his problem?
A   His boss is unfair to him.
B   He has been ill.
C   He has too much to do.

[pause]

tone

Man: I don't know what Jim's got to grumble about. My workload has doubled in the past year and I still manage. He's not doing any different from when he arrived, as far as I can see.

Woman: Yeah, but he's not as energetic as you are. Well, no one is. But Mr Craddock doesn't tell me off when I get a bit behind, he's very understanding with me. But with Jim, he goes on and on.

Man: I haven't noticed it, but you're probably right. I wonder why he does it?

[pause]

tone

[The recording is repeated.]

[pause]

Question 8   Eight
Listen to this woman phoning a travel agent. What does she want to do?
A   *cancel her booking*
B   *postpone her holiday*
C   *change her destination*

[pause]

tone

Woman: … on the fourth of June … Yes. Amsterdam, Holland … Now, my problem is, my brother's there, and he was supposed to be fixing accommodation for me but he has a problem with his work right now and he asked me to reserve it from here … Yeah, well what it is, I don't really want to spend my vacation going around the city alone. So I wanted to ask you whether it would cost a lot to alter the flight, say till later in the summer, when maybe he'll be freer, and we might even get to visit a few more places?

[pause]

tone

[The recording is repeated.]

[pause]

That's the end of Part One.
Now turn to Part Two.

PART 2   *You will hear an interview about sports facilities. For questions 9 to 18 fill in the answers on the questionnaire. You now have forty-five seconds in which to look at Part Two.*

[pause]

tone

Woman:	Excuse me, I'm doing some research on behalf of the local Sports Committee. Would you mind answering a few questions?
Man:	Well, if it won't take too long, OK.
Woman:	Thanks. Um, first of all, are you a local resident?
Man:	Well, more or less. It's just south of the ring road.
Woman:	Oh, right, so I could put you down as 'in the suburbs'?
Man:	Yes.
Woman:	And are you a student, or …?
Man:	I've just started work actually. I'm a librarian.
Woman:	Oh, yes? And do you use the public swimming pool regularly?
Man:	About once a week, I suppose, though it might be less in winter.
Woman:	Right. And what do you think about the hours it opens? Should it be open later, for example?
Man:	Yes, I think it should. I'd use it more often if I could go later in the evening, and I think some of my friends would too.
Woman:	Uh-huh. How about the cost? Are the charges reasonable?
Man:	Well, I can afford them now I'm earning, but it's not cheap, and considering it's not particularly luxurious, I think they're a bit too high, really. Especially for school kids and families.
Woman:	Mm. So you think the facilities could be improved?
Man:	Yes, they definitely need modernising. Apart from the odd coat of paint, they haven't changed since I was a kid. When I was in Birmingham the other week I went to a pool there and I couldn't believe the difference.
Woman:	Is there anything in particular you'd like to see added?
Man:	There definitely aren't enough showers! Anyone can tell you that!
Woman:	Yes, they do! And um, do you think there are any other sports which should be catered for locally but which aren't at the moment?
Man:	Well, the sports centre is good, although it's not all that big, but like most towns you haven't really got access to anywhere for athletics unless you travel to somewhere really big. And that's no good for kids who want to train regularly.
Woman:	Yes, I agree. And there's no coaching available either, once they get beyond a certain level, is there? Anyway, we must get on. If there could be some modernisation to the pool, or other sports facilities could be improved, do you have any opinion about how that should be paid for?
Man:	Well, that's the problem, isn't it? Personally, I wouldn't mind paying a bit more tax, if it would actually get spent on the right things. But I'm young and single and I can afford to say that. Really I think the Sports Committee need to get local businesses involved. That's probably the only practical possibility.
Woman:	Right. And – I've nearly done – there've been suggestions that some groups should be able to use the pool without charge. Do you agree with this, and if so who should that be?
Man:	I visited Australia last year and I discovered that where I was staying, pensioners could get in for nothing. I think that's a really good idea. And long term it could save on doctor's bills, couldn't it?
Woman:	I suppose it might. Well thank you very much for your help.
Man:	That's OK. Bye.
Woman:	Goodbye … Excuse me, I'm doing some research on behalf of the local Sports …

[pause]

tone

Now you'll hear Part Two again.

[The recording is repeated.]

[pause]

That's the end of Part Two.
Now turn to Part Three.

PART 3   *You will hear five people talking to someone they have just met. For questions 19 to 23, choose which of the people A to F each speaker is talking to. Use the letters only once. There is one extra letter which you do not need to use. You now have 30 seconds in which to look at Part Three.*

[pause]

tone

First woman:	I've never done anything like this before, have you?

Second woman:	Er, no.

First woman: I mean I always thought that organised tours meant bunches of foreigners buzzing around with cameras saying, 'If it's Wednesday this must be Copenhagen'. But with such a small number you don't really feel we're tourists in that sense, do you?

[pause]

Woman: Come to join the madhouse? This is my little corner here, and I think you'll find you're just round here.

Man: Oh, thanks.

Woman: Now I expect you'll want a few minutes to sort your stuff out, then I'll take you round and show you where everything is. OK?

Man: Yes. Thank you very much.

[pause]

First man: Have you ever been on one of these before? My boss says it'll make all the difference. Well, I think she hopes it will! I'm hopeless at time management.

Second man: Oh?

First man: Quite posh sort of place this, isn't it? I suppose that's the chap who's going to tell us what to do. It'd better be good. It's costing our companies quite a bit to send us.

Second man: Mm.

[pause]

First woman: I do hope you're going to like it here. We were so glad when we heard it'd been sold. It's not nice being near an empty place for so long. We've always found people to be very friendly, and you know, we help each other out with little jobs around the place. You're not married, are you?

Second woman: Er, well.

First woman: Well, do drop round any time if you want a hand with anything, or you need to know where to go for anything.

Second woman: Thanks.

[pause]

Man:	Well, that's about it really. I hope you'll find it suits you. As I said, any queries, just call me and I'll see what I can sort out.
Woman:	Thanks.
Man:	And if you do decide to use the little room as an office, just let me know and I'll get the bed out and I'll bring you a desk.
Woman:	Right, thanks.
Man:	Anyway, I expect you want to get your stuff sorted out, so if you just give me your cheque for the first month, I'll hand over your keys and leave you to it.

[pause]

tone

Now you'll hear Part Three again.

[The recording is repeated.]

[pause]

That's the end of Part Three.
Now turn to Part Four.

PART 4   *You will hear a discussion between Andy and Sharon about advertising their small business. For questions 24 to 30, decide which of the statements are true and which are false and write T for True or F for False in the box provided. You now have forty-five seconds in which to look at Part Four.*

[pause]

tone

Andy:	What was it you wanted to discuss, Sharon?
Sharon:	Well, it's this thing about advertising, Andy. I think we need to get information about ourselves across to possible customers, otherwise we're just not going to increase sales.
Andy:	OK. We both accept we're going to have to spend more in order to get business. So, let's look at the situation. We've already paid out quite a bit for that advertisement in *Local Business News*. Everyone says it was a great little advertisement, they all like it when we show it to them. Do you think it was worth it?
Sharon:	That's the problem. We don't really know. But I suspect not. Because we need to reach the guys working in the offices, staff, whatever, and that magazine lies about in reception areas for bored customers.
Andy:	Yeah, I'm sure you're right. The woman who persuaded us to take that ad out was just after what she could get. We shouldn't have listened to her. What I think we should do is advertise in the local paper.
Sharon:	Oh, come on Andy, that rag!
Andy:	Yeah, I rang them and we thought that on the same page as jobs are advertised, under Business Services. So people who're, you know, just flicking through to see if there are any better jobs going, you know, everyone does it, they see this little ad, and think, Yeah, that'd be handy for us.
Sharon:	OK. Could we afford it every day?

Andy:　I thought every Thursday. That's when the most job adverts are in. They said they'd give quite a good discount if we have a long series, say for a few months.

Sharon:　Right, that's good. Anything else? I mean, what if we got some leaflets printed and stuck them through letterboxes?

Andy:　It could be very effective, but I think there's one big disadvantage.

Sharon:　Oh?

Andy:　Well, it'd take ages to deliver them all. We've got little enough time as it is.

Sharon:　But if we paid someone else to do it?

Andy:　Who, for example? It'd be too small scale for them to want to do. Anyway, we couldn't afford a professional firm.

Sharon:　Yeah, well, I'm not so sure of that. But anyway, what about getting some students to do it? It'd be a great way for them to earn a bit of money.

Andy:　Yeah, and I know just what'd happen. They'd stick the whole lot through the first five doors and push off home. We'd never be able to keep a check on them.

Sharon:　Oh, I don't know. Well, perhaps you're right. OK, let's look at the figures for the newspaper and then see whether we could afford anything else.

[pause]

tone

Now you'll hear Part Four again.

[The recording is repeated.]

[pause]

That is the end of Part Four.
There'll now be a pause of five minutes for you to copy your answers onto the separate answer sheet.
I'll remind you when there's one minute left, so that you're sure to finish in time.

[pause]

You have one more minute left.

[pause]

That's the end of the test. Please stop now. Your supervisor will now collect all the question papers and answer sheets.
Goodbye.

Test 3 Key

Paper 1 Reading

Part 1
1 E   2 G   3 C   4 H   5 A   6 F   7 B

Part 2
8 C   9 D   10 A   11 C   12 B   13 A   14 C   15 B

Part 3
16 G   17 D   18 A   19 C   20 B   21 F

Part 4
22 and 23 A/B   24 D   25 and 26 A/D   27 B   28 C
29 and 30 A/C   31 A   32 A   33 C   34 B   35 A
(Where there are two possible answers, these are interchangeable.)

Paper 2 Writing

Part 1 – Plan

<u>letter to friend</u>

why I'm writing

describe hotel
- on sea front
- run by friendly family
- good food
- 2 pools

describe my holiday
- sailing – really good
- coach trip – interesting
- evenings – plenty to do

hope we can go together next year – sure we'd enjoy it

Paper 3 Use of English

Award one mark for each correct answer, except in Part 3, where two marks are available, divided up as shown, for each answer.

Correct spelling is essential throughout. Ignore omission or abuse of capital letters. No half marks.

Part 1

1 C   2 B   3 B   4 C   5 A   6 B   7 D   8 B   9 A
10 C   11 A   12 D   13 B   14 A   15 C

Part 2

16 to   17 an/the   18 make   19 with/under/in   20 what
21 at   22 as   23 while/when/if   24 both   25 but/whereas
26 is   27 this   28 than   29 not   30 can

Part 3

31 isn't/'s/is not worth (1) asking (1)
32 would not/wouldn't/did not/didn't let/refused to let (1) him buy/get (1)
33 where she had left (1) her (1)
34 way (1) John behaved (1)
35 if you (1) had not/hadn't lent (1)
36 no notice (1) of his doctor's (1)
37 in addition (1) to writing (1)
38 during/of (1) his childhood (1)
39 don't we/not (1) go to/go and visit (1)
40 had difficulty (in) (1) concentrating on (1)

Part 4

41 a   42 ✓   43 near   44 one   45 they   46 ✓   47 the
48 away   49 about   50 since   51 in   52 an   53 ✓
54 no   55 much

Part 5

56 width   57 height   58 disagreement   59 pressure
60 popularity   61 Unfortunately   62 wonderful   63 requirements
64 inhabitants   65 rarely

Paper 4 Listening

Part 1

1 A   2 A   3 A   4 B   5 A   6 C   7 C   8 B

Part 2

9 Thursday(s)   10 gallery   11 photography   12 print technology
13 model making   14 academic secretary   15 third year
16 stationery/notebooks   17 administration assistant   18 Department Head

Part 3
19 D   20 A   21 E   22 C   23 B

Part 4
24 C   25 A   26 B   27 B   28 A   29 C   30 B

Tapescript   *First Certificate Practice Test Three. Paper Four. Listening. Hello, I'm going to give you the instructions for this test. I'll introduce each part of the test and give you time to look at the questions. At the start of each piece, you'll hear this sound:*

tone

You'll hear each piece twice.
Remember, while you're listening, write your answers on the question paper. You'll have time at the end of the test to copy your answers onto the separate answer sheet.
The tape will now be stopped. Please ask any questions now, because you must not speak during the test.

[pause]

PART 1   *Now, open your question paper and look at Part One. You'll hear people talking in eight different situations. For questions 1 to 8, choose the best answer, A, B or C.*

Question 1   One
You are visiting a trade exhibition when you hear a speaker at one of the stands. What is he demonstrating?
A a watch
B a lock
C a burglar alarm

[pause]

tone

Salesman: … and now I do up the strap, see, it clicks in and it's securely held. That won't slip, whatever you do, and as I said, you can't really damage it. Water's no problem, and if you leave if off and someone else tries to walk off with it, he'll soon regret it because of the high-pitched whistle which only you can de-activate …

[pause]

tone

[The recording is repeated.]

[pause]

Question 2 *Two*
This girl is talking about a party. What was it like?
A boring
B too crowded
C noisy

[pause]

tone

Girl: No, I wouldn't bother. The last one was useless. She'd made all this food, like she was expecting about fifty people, and then hardly anyone turned up, and her music system is useless, so unless you were next to it, you practically couldn't hear the music well enough to dance even though it was turned right up. It was dead dull, basically.

[pause]

tone

[The recording is repeated.]

[pause]

Question 3 *Three*
Listen to this hotel receptionist talking on the phone. Who is she talking to?
A a friend
B a guest
C her employer

[pause]

tone

Hotel
receptionist: … row about eleven o'clock. So old George went on up, thinking it was a burglar, and he was going to march him off … Anyway it was this Mr Hardiman, he'd locked himself out and he was trying to force the door! You should've seen George's face … That's right. And all the heads popping round their doors. Were we grateful the boss was away for the night!

[pause]

tone

[The recording is repeated.]

[pause]

Question 4 *Four*
You hear this advertisement on the radio. Who is it aimed at?
A people who have plenty of money
B people who might borrow money
C people who need to save money

[pause]

tone

Woman: Close your eyes and picture yourself in a beautiful dining-room. The table is dark wood, polished to a deep shine. The silver and glassware are reflected in the beautiful mirror hanging above the sideboard. Long curtains in rich brocade frame the window. Now, open your eyes and look around you. Fancy a change? It could all be yours with a loan from Home Finance Services. Just ring 0800 2323, that's 0800 2323 for details of our very competitive rates.

[pause]

tone

[The recording is repeated.]

[pause]

Question 5   *Five*
Listen to these students talking about their holiday work. Where are they
working?
A a library
B an office
C a shop

[pause]

tone

Student 1: … so then he just came up to me and said, 'Isn't it time you knew how to classify reference books?' He can be really mean.
Student 2: I know, and he makes you do the evenings when there's no one else there so you can't really stop people taking things out which aren't for external loans, and then he blames you because things are missing.
Student 1: So, I said, 'But at least I understand how the computer works!'
Student 2: I bet that got him.
Student 1: Yeah. He went all red and didn't speak to me for hours.

[pause]

tone

[The recording is repeated.]

[pause]

Question 6   *Six*
Listen to this man. Where has he been?
A to the gym
B to the dentist
C to the barber

[pause]

tone

Man: Just don't ask! It was the usual story. You go in and say, 'Look, I just want a trim, tidy up a few straggly ends'. You know. Next thing you know you're imprisoned in this chair while some madman is let loose on you and you end up looking like this! No, it's not funny.

[pause]

tone

[The recording is repeated.]

[pause]

Question 7 *Seven*
You hear this woman talking on the radio. What is she discussing?
A *music*
B *a picture*
C *architecture*

[pause]

tone

Woman: ... I've got nothing against simple forms. Some of the most dramatic views in the world are created by a harmonious arrangement of very simple forms. That's fine. But this, this isn't simplicity, it's, it's flatness. It's painted in the dullest shades which are quite inappropriate to this climate. It's out of tune with its surroundings, and worst of all, I suspect, it will be unpleasant to work in as well as being an eyesore for people who have to pass by it every day.

[pause]

tone

[The recording is repeated.]

[pause]

Question 8 *Eight*
You hear this man talking to a shop assistant. Why is he annoyed?
A *His pen has leaked in his pocket.*
B *His pen has been repaired recently.*
C *His pen was very expensive.*

[pause]

tone

Man: Look, I realise it's not exactly the top of the range – it wasn't particularly expensive or anything, but you had it in for a repair only a fortnight ago and that cost far more than it should have done and then yesterday it started leaking when I was using it and made the most incredible mess. If it had done that in my pocket, it could have ruined an expensive suit. It really isn't on, you know!

[pause]

tone

[The recording is repeated.]

[pause]

That's the end of Part One.
Now turn to Part Two.

PART 2 *You will hear a teacher telling new students about their course. For questions 9 to 18 listen to what she says and complete the notes. You now have thirty seconds in which to look at Part Two.*

[pause]

tone

Teacher: Well, I'm very glad to welcome you all to the practical module of our Design course at the beginning of a new year. As you've no doubt realised, we have people here from years one to three, and we find that as most of the work is in small groups or individually-based, this works out pretty well, even though we're a bit short of space. Now I'm going to go through some administrative stuff and then we'll get on to project planning. So, first of all, hm, we're in the Studio here every afternoon except one, so we do have a sort of base, which is quite nice, but once a week we have to move out, that's into Room 51, which is on Thursdays. It's a bit of a nuisance, because it's not as big as in here, but we manage somehow. And on Fridays you can use the big space over the back of the hall, which is called the Gallery, for private study if you want to spread out a bit. That's only on Fridays though, I'm afraid. Now as far as extra courses go. You should've already selected these, and the days for them are as follows: um, Mondays is the only day when the darkroom is free, so that's photography. Tuesdays John Howard comes in here to take the sessions on Print Technology, and Wednesdays I'm here for Model-making. Now if you haven't selected your options for this term, you need to get a move on. When we finish now, I'll be showing you round the rest of the department and you can get a form from the academic secretary on the way. Oh, you also need to get one if you want to do the full-day course, which is on Saturdays on Computer-aided Design. But that only applies to you third-year students, of course, and you know where the office is.

   Now, that's nearly all, except a reminder to you all that we provide all the equipment you need for practical work, including card and photographic papers, but you must bring your own stationery. You should have proper notebooks, and we don't expect to have to find bits of paper for you to make notes on when you forget them. And, lastly, about absence. If you're not well, if it's just a couple of days, you can phone the administration assistant, ask him to pass a message on to this department. If it's more than a couple of days, you must send a written explanation to the Department Head otherwise you could be penalised in your course grade for absence without permission. OK? Well you have been warned. Now, for you new guys, let's go and look round the rest of the place. The rest of you no doubt have things to be getting on with.

[pause]

tone

Now you'll hear Part Two again.

[The recording is repeated.]

[pause]

That's the end of Part Two.
Now turn to Part Three.

PART 3   *You will hear five people saying thank you. For questions 19 to 23, choose*
which of A to F each speaker is talking about. Use the letters only once. There
is one extra letter which you do not need to use. You now have 30 seconds in
which to look at Part Three.

[pause]

tone

Man: This is not an occasion where it is easy for me to know what to say. I realised of course that I wouldn't get away without some kind of little memento. After all, we've been together a long time and I know what a generous bunch you are. But I had absolutely no idea that it was going to be something like this. It's quite magnificent. Really, I'm lost for words. Except that I'm beginning to think I'll have to move house. It's so grand it'll make the rest of the place look terrible in comparison! Thank you all very, very much.

[pause]

Woman: I just called to say thank you. I've just had my results. And I know I'd never have done so well if you hadn't been pushing me this last term! … Well, it's nice of you to say so, but honestly, I never even found the subject interesting until I got into your class.

[pause]

Man: Anyway, thanks very much for putting me on to them. They were just the right people for the job. I don't know why nobody here had heard of them. But as the boss says, 'If you want to know anything about anything, all you have to do is ask Carole! She's got all the answers.' Many thanks, and let me know if ever I can help you out some way.

[pause]

Man: Well, I certainly owe you one this time. Thank you very much indeed for telling me what might happen. It would have been a total disaster if I'd let them take it away. I think you've just saved me a lot of money. And listen, if I can do anything for you, all you have to do is name it!

[pause]

Woman: I'd like to take this opportunity to thank all of you for your hard work over the past few months. I don't need to tell you but, er, I want you to be sure that I know too, that without you guys here doing all the routine, and not so routine, work, and doing it without much understanding from outside, so that I could get on with my stuff – well, I wouldn't have achieved anything. It was a tough job for all of us and I won't forget what you've all done for me, I promise.

[pause]

tone

Now you'll hear Part Three again.

[The recording is repeated.]

[pause]

That's the end of Part Three.
Now turn to Part Four.

PART 4   *You will hear a radio discussion about a wildlife park. For questions 24 to 30,*
decide which of the choices, A, B or C is the correct answer. You now have
one minute in which to look at Part Four.

[pause]

tone

Gary: Now, I have with me here this evening two people who are both very interested in the
future of Glenside Park. Helen, you represent the management committee of the park,
and Ian (Good evening.), you represent the residents of the village of South Glen which
lies just beyond the park and through which the main road into the park passes. I
understand that the residents aren't too happy about some of your plans, Helen. Could
you just give us an outline of what exactly these are?

Helen: Well, yes, I'm very happy to explain because I think part of the problem that has arisen
is that some people in South Glen have got the wrong idea about our plans. Once they
see what we're trying to do here, I think they'll agree it's a very sensible way forward.

Ian: We see perfectly well, we just don't happen to think you're right ...

Gary: OK, Ian, Ian, you'll have your say in a minute. Now, Helen, what exactly is it you're
proposing?

Helen: Yes. As you know, Glenside has two problems at the moment. First, we're short of
money, and second we've got too many people wandering about in parts of the park
where animals, especially the birds, are trying to raise their young, disturbing them and
sometimes causing the young to be left by their parents, so the staff have to try and
save them by raising them by hand, which takes up precious time and, of course, is
expensive.

Gary: So what do you want to do?

Helen: We think the best way to raise money would be to have more visitors to the park who'd
be prepared to pay to see the animals.

Ian: But that's ridiculous! (No, it's not.) On the one hand you're accusing people of upsetting
the animals, and then the next minute you're saying you want more people wandering
about.

Helen: No, the point is that at the moment, people walk all over the place, they don't keep to
the roads, they scare the birds, and there's a constant danger that a fire might be
started and we wouldn't be able to do anything because we wouldn't know until it was
too late.

Ian: Wait a minute, wait a minute. What are you talking about? People from the village would
no more want to damage the park than you do!

Helen: I don't mean they'd do it on purpose. But there are such things as accidents.

Ian: Oh, come on – how many fires have you had in the last ten years?

Helen: I'm not saying we have, just that we might. Now, what we want is to have fixed routes
through the park, so that visitors can be taken through and have things pointed out and
explained ...

Ian: And where might these people park, may one enquire? Because it won't help relations with the village if all the roads through it are blocked with tourist cars and buses and we can't even walk through the woods where our parents and grandparents have been able to walk for generations, without paying for the honour!

Gary: He has got a point there, I think, Helen. After all, it would be quite a revolutionary plan, wouldn't it?

Helen: But people can't expect something for nothing. No, they could get tickets for a season, so they wouldn't have to queue. But they'd have to learn to respect the wildlife.

Ian: Look, tell me one example of serious harm which has been done by a local resident. We've been here for years before you turned up. If we didn't respect the land and the living things on it, it wouldn't be here for people like you to move in and start making profits out of. What have you ever done for South Glen?

Gary: OK, OK, OK, well, well, I can see that we're going to have a lot more discussion about this before the plans are carried out. (Yeah.) There is going to be a public meeting next Wednesday at South Glen Community Centre and I'm sure it'll be well-attended. Now, I think perhaps we need some music to calm us down, so here's a little tune I'm sure …

[pause]

tone

Now you'll hear Part Four again.

[The recording is repeated.]

[pause]

That is the end of Part Four.
There'll now be a pause of five minutes for you to copy your answers onto the separate answer sheet.
I'll remind you when there's one minute left, so that you're sure to finish in time.

[pause]

You have one more minute left.

[pause]

That's the end of the test. Please stop now. Your supervisor will now collect all the question papers and answer sheets.
Goodbye.

Test 4 Key

Paper 1 Reading

Part 1
1 D   2 F   3 A   4 H   5 B   6 G   7 E

Part 2
8 D   9 D   10 A   11 A   12 B   13 C   14 B

Part 3
15 E   16 F   17 B   18 G   19 C   20 H   21 A

Part 4
22 and 23 A/C   24 D   25 C   26 B   27 A   **28 and 29** B/D
30 A   31 D   32 A   **33 and 34** B/D   35 E
(Where there are two possible answers, these are interchangeable.)

Paper 2 Writing

Part 1 – Plan

> <u>letter to Mr Stevens</u> (N.B. not a friend)
>
> why I'm writing – apologise: can't meet train because late class
>
> best way for him
> either
> - taxi (where to find one)
> - ask for college (tell driver where it is – between hospital & fire station)
> or
> - bus (stop closer to station)
> - ask for hospital – walk back to college – not far
>
> hope he doesn't mind/has good journey
> all looking forward to his talk

171

Paper 3 Use of English

Award one mark for each correct answer, except in Part 3, where two marks are available, divided up as shown, for each answer.

Correct spelling is essential throughout. Ignore omission or abuse of capital letters. No half marks.

Part 1

1 C   2 D   3 B   4 B   5 D   6 A   7 C   8 B   9 A
10 D   11 C   12 B   13 D   14 C   15 B

Part 2

16 another *(allow* each/every); [*not* a]   17 of   18 a   19 it   20 for   21 who   22 became [*not* was]   23 would   24 By   25 have   26 may/might   27 which/that   28 capable
29 Until/Till   30 in

Part 3

31 (that) Brenda (1) waited/(should) wait (1)
   or to Brenda (1) she should wait/(that) she wait(ed); [Brenda to wait = 0]
32 not (1) waking/getting up (1)
33 first time (1) I have/I've eaten (1)
34 managed (1) to arrest (1)
35 ought to have (1) written (1)
36 has (1) such small handwriting (that) (1)
37 have to/must (1) be picked up (1)
38 regret telling him (1) our plans (1)
39 everyone's surprise (,) (1) Geoff left (1)
40 I was to blame (1) for (1)

Part 4

41 ✓   42 still   43 so   44 a   45 ✓   46 as   47 the
48 when   49 for   50 it   51 also   52 ✓   53 well
54 ourselves   55 ✓

Part 5

56 speaking   57 preparation   58 encouraged   59 ensure
60 correctly   61 liking   62 tastiest   63 dangerous
64 importance   65 heavily

Paper 4 Listening

Part 1

1 A   2 C   3 A   4 C   5 B   6 A   7 A   8 B

Part 2

9 (beautiful, sandy) beach   10 medium-sized   11 drive/car

12 June 13 (enormous) cliffs 14 tiny 15 coach 16 model village
17 drive/car 18 winter

Part 3
19 D 20 A 21 E 22 B 23 C

Part 4
24 A 25 C 26 C 27 A 28 C 29 S 30 S

Tapescript *First Certificate Practice Test Four. Paper Four. Listening. Hello, I'm going to give you the instructions for this test. I'll introduce each part of the test and give you time to look at the questions. At the start of each piece, you'll hear this sound.*

tone

You'll hear each piece twice.
Remember, while you're listening, write your answers on the question paper. You'll have time at the end of the test to copy your answers onto the separate answer sheet.
The tape will now be stopped. Please ask any questions now, because you must not speak during the test.

[pause]

PART 1 *Now open your question paper and look at Part One.*
You'll hear people talking in eight different situations. For questions 1 to 8, choose the best answer, A, B or C.

Question 1 *One*
These women are talking about a colleague. What do they feel about his behaviour?
A It was typical of him.
B It had improved.
C It reminded them of someone else.

[pause]

tone

First woman: Well, it was hardly surprising really, was it? D'you remember how he went on when we tried to change the booking system?
Second woman: You'd have thought he'd invented it himself the way he was carrying on.
First woman: This time he went right to the Section Manager. He's a real pain about that sort of thing.
Second woman: He doesn't seem to be able to see that we're only trying to make things work better.
First woman: Exactly. I just can't get through to him at all.

[pause]

tone

[The recording is repeated.]

173

[pause]

Question 2   *Two*
This man is talking about a sports event. What happened to his team?
A   They won.
B   They did better than he'd hoped.
C   They were very unlucky.

[pause]

tone

Man: It was incredible! We'd come right up through the league from the qualifying round. I'd always known we'd had it in us if we could just get it together. And we'd been really lucky when Mike moved into the area and joined us. It made a lot of difference. And then, there we were all set for the final, everyone in top form and three men had to pull out for silly little reasons. I couldn't believe my ears when they phoned, one after another. From then on, I knew what to expect. Even the winners said luck had been on their side.

[pause]

tone

[The recording is repeated.]

[pause]

Question 3   *Three*
Listen to this man telephoning someone about his washing machine. Who is he talking to?
A   an engineer
B   a friend
C   the shop he bought it from

[pause]

tone

Man: … been in touch with them already and they said it's not up to them, because the guarantee doesn't cover it. So I was wondering whether it might be the sort of thing you could handle? … I don't suppose you could give me any idea of what the charge might be? … Yes, I see. The thing is, I've got some friends coming round this weekend and um … Oh, that'd be great!

[pause]

tone

[The recording is repeated.]

[pause]

Question 4   *Four*
You switch on the radio and hear this report. Where is it coming from?
A *a market*
B *a concert hall*
C *a racetrack*

[pause]

tone

Sports reporter: And there's a tremendous crowd here today – everyone's milling about, looking very excited. There's laughter and music and lots of chatter. I've been talking to some of the people around me and there's no doubt that there's a fair amount of money changing hands as well. And now we'll go over to Arnold Burns who's been watching the runners coming up to the start.

[pause]

tone

[The recording is repeated.]

[pause]

Question 5   *Five*
You hear this man talking about his bad back. How did he injure it?
A *in a road accident*
B *by lifting something*
C *in a fight*

[pause]

tone

Man: It's not much better. Thanks for asking. I wouldn't mind so much if I hadn't been trying to help someone else. You know, John was there, struggling with this damn great case and I thought, oh, I can't leave him to cope on his own, so I went over and said, 'Let's get it up onto the wheels', and I was sort of lifting, and he was pushing, and suddenly I just felt something go in my back and that was it.

[pause]

tone

[The recording is repeated.]

[pause]

Question 6   *Six*
You overhear these people talking about a book. What sort of book is it?
A *a guidebook*
B *a history book*
C *a novel*

[pause]

tone

Man:	... so I asked him what he thought, 'cause he'd been there.
Woman:	And so?
Man:	Well, he said most of the descriptions were quite accurate. You know, the old bits of the town, they really do look like that even now. But the factual details about good value for money, he said, they're not really aimed at people like us.
Woman:	How do you mean?
Man:	Well, it's written for older people really, so what he says is reasonably cheap, is really quite expensive, and when he says some old inn or something is 'adequate', we'd find it really comfortable.
Woman:	Perhaps I'd better see if I can find something more suitable.

[pause]

tone

[The recording is repeated.]

[pause]

Question 7   *Seven*
Listen to this woman who has just arrived at a meeting. Why is she late?
A   The weather was bad.
B   There was a traffic jam.
C   She crashed her car.

[pause]

tone

Woman:	I'm so sorry. I do hope you haven't been waiting to begin. It was just after I left Oxford, there was this tremendously heavy rain and all the traffic had to slow right down, you couldn't see a thing. I was convinced I was going to hit something. Anyway, I'm really sorry.

[pause]

tone

[The recording is repeated.]

[pause]

Question 8   *Eight*
At the sports club you hear these people discussing an exercise. What is its purpose?
A   to help you lose weight
B   to make you relax
C   to strengthen the stomach muscles

[pause]

tone

Man:	So, was the class any use?
Woman:	It was pretty tiring! We did do some quite good things though. There was one where you had to lie on your stomach, and very gently move your arms from above your head down to your sides.
Man:	Hardly very energetic!
Woman:	But you feel very sort of calm afterwards. All the tension goes out of your shoulders. At least that's the idea, apparently.

[pause]

tone

[The recording is repeated.]

[pause]

That's the end of Part One.
Now turn to Part Two.

PART 2   *You will hear part of a radio programme about holidays. For questions 9 to 18, complete the grid. You now have thirty seconds in which to look at Part Two.*

[pause]

tone

Presenter:	Hello and welcome to the Holiday Spot. Today we have reports on three contrasting places, all within a couple of hours of the capital. And first we have Gabrielle, who's been to Eastingham.
Gabrielle:	Yes, well, I must admit I thought I was the unlucky one, getting Eastingham, but in fact I was really pleasantly surprised. I thought the main attraction would be night clubs and fast food bars. In fact it's just a medium-sized town with an old-fashioned sea front, and most of the visitors are there for the absolutely beautiful sandy beach, which is actually more impressive in reality than on the postcards. I went by road, as it didn't occur to me that I could go by train, and I must say that although it might have saved me half an hour, it would have meant quite a long walk at the other end, as the station is on the inland side of the town. Also, for a day trip, a car's a must, as the last train is a very slow one. And I had no trouble parking even though I was there in August. I was told that June is ideal, when the weather is most likely to be sunshine but the crowds haven't got too bad. Actually I suspect that Eastingham's idea of really crowded would be some resorts' idea of pleasantly lively. Um, for a relaxed day in the traditional style, Eastingham's just the place.
Presenter:	Thanks, Gabrielle. Now we turn to Josh, who's been sampling the delights of Brant, just ten miles along the coast.
Josh:	Yes, I've just returned from an amazing weekend. Brant is a tiny place with several excellent homely guest houses and visitors come here because it's a great base for a walking holiday. Its most exciting feature is the enormous cliffs which rear up above the sea. It's not too difficult to reach from the city, only about an hour and half's drive by coach and these go most days. It's not really a good idea to take your own car, even though the roads aren't bad, because the parking space is very restricted and during the day it's expensive. But a great place to get the traffic fumes out of your lungs.

Presenter: Thank you Josh. You certainly sound refreshed. And lastly, we hear from Catherine, who's been on a day trip to Faresey. I believe you took some friends with you, Catherine?

Catherine: Well, I'd heard that Faresey boasted an attraction which was popular with children from eight to eighty, so I took my neighbour Tom, who's twelve, and his granddad, Alec, who's seventy. And, well, the day was a roaring success. Faresey is the home of a model railway, but what really pulls in the crowds is that you can spend hours going round an entire model village, complete with market, workshops and houses, all based on Faresey in the nineteenth century. I was fascinated by it, and so were my friends. I had been worried that there wouldn't be enough to keep Tom occupied, but the working model machines really hooked him. Faresey itself is a pleasant small town, and the model village is something which you can't help being interested by. It's easy to get to if you drive, as it's just ten minutes from the motorway, about forty minutes altogether from here. And it's open all the year round. In fact, I'd recommend it as a good day out during winter rather than summer, as you could still be there and back in daylight and the crowds might be thinner, so you wouldn't have to wait for a clear view of the models. Not that that's a great problem, even in summer, but you do have to be a bit patient at some of the best bits.

Presenter: Well, it sounds as though you've all had a good time. Many thanks. And now to our foreign holiday slot. Here's Jenny …

[pause]

tone

Now you'll hear Part Two again.

[The recording is repeated.]

[pause]

That's the end of Part Two.
Now turn to Part Three.

PART 3 *You will hear five people talking about clothes. For questions 19 to 23, choose from the list A to F what each speaker is talking about. Use the letters only once. There is one extra letter which you do not need to use. You now have 30 seconds in which to look at Part Three.*

[pause]

tone

Woman: And now here is Patrick. This is beautifully cut in fine wool with hand-sewn detail on the sleeves and a flattering pleat at the waistline of the trousers. The jacket lining is of silk, making it wonderfully comfortable. This is an absolute must for winter which you'll still be wearing next spring. It's available in a range of colours, both classic and more adventurous.

[pause]

Woman: I've had it for years. Actually I think it was my grandfather's. I expect he used to wear it on expeditions. It keeps the sun out of your eyes without making your head hot. Everyone laughs at illustrations of nineteenth-century costume, but all the same they did get some things right. And this is one of them. Well, as far as I'm concerned anyway.

[pause]

Man: Well, it was pouring with rain, as you know, and when we got there I had to take my shoes off because they were absolutely soaked. It was so embarrassing. There was this great hole with my toe sticking out. I'm sure it wasn't there when I was getting dressed. It must have caught on the shoe lining and then just spread. Well, what could I do? I just laughed!

[pause]

Woman: Where does he find them? Last week he had on, I'm not joking, an open-necked, orange and pink nylon striped one. He looked like a garden chair. Jeremy said it gave him a headache looking at it all day. I don't know what the customers make of it. You'd think he'd get cold in those short sleeves too.

[pause]

Man: Yeah, I'm very pleased with it really. It's big enough to go over anything, it's really warm and it looks smart enough. I never used to bother when I drove to work, but now I'm using the train I needed something to keep out the wind and rain. That's why I have it so long. It keeps my knees dry too.

[pause]

tone

Now you'll hear Part Three again.

[The recording is repeated.]

[pause]

That's the end of Part Three.
Now turn to Part Four.

PART 4   *You will hear two friends discussing evening study courses. For questions 24 to 30, decide which course each statement refers to. Mark A for Art, or C for Computers or S for Spanish. You now have forty-five seconds in which to look at Part Four.*

[pause]

tone

Tracy: Hey, Polly, how's it going?

Polly: Hi, Tracy. Hey, I went into the Institute on my way home today to find out about evening classes. They've got some very good courses planned this year.

Tracy: Oh, did you get a leaflet?

Polly: No, they're re-printing them. But some are the same as last year, and I made a couple of notes.

Tracy: I'm not sure I really want to bother this year. It's such a drag turning out again after you get in in the evening. And that painting course had so many people in it that you couldn't really get any individual help.

Polly: Yes, well they've decided to limit the numbers this year, so if you want to do it you have to book a place. I can understand why, I suppose. Anyway I don't know, but I wonder whether I ought to do the computing really. It might be useful. I mean if I was going for promotion.

Tracy: But would it be advanced enough for you, Polly? You already do quite a lot of that sort of thing, don't you?

Polly: Oh, I think so. The woman who runs it is supposed to be very good. She's not just a programmer, she's a trained teacher as well.

Tracy: Well, it's up to you of course. Sounds like my idea of hell, at the end of a day's work. I just want something relaxing.

Polly: But Tracy, I think you really ought to do something, even if it's just the same one as last year.

Tracy: But then I'd have to pay for materials. That's another reason I don't think I want to do it again. I can't afford more than the minimum.

Polly: Well, why don't you try Spanish? It'd be easy for you, Tracy, knowing Italian, and it'd be really useful on holiday.

Tracy: Mm. Don't the language courses last two terms? I don't know I want to tie myself up for that long.

Polly: Er, I don't think so, no. That's the computer course. But they're pretty intensive so you really get through a lot in a short time.

Tracy: If it's so good, why don't you try it yourself?

Polly: I'd like to, it's just I ought to consider my career and I don't have time for both.

Tracy: Oh, well. Let's think about it over the weekend.

Polly: All right.

[pause]

tone

Now you'll hear Part Four again.

[The recording is repeated.]

[pause]

That is the end of Part Four.
There'll now be a pause of five minutes for you to copy your answers onto the separate answer sheet.
I'll remind you when there's one minute left, so that you're sure to finish in time.

[pause]

You have one more minute left.

[pause]

That's the end of the test. Please stop now. Your supervisor will now collect all the question papers and answer sheets. Goodbye.

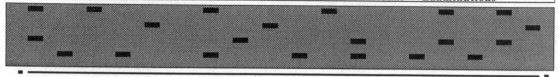

CAMBRIDGE
EXAMINATIONS, CERTIFICATES AND DIPLOMAS
ENGLISH AS A FOREIGN LANGUAGE

University of Cambridge
Local Examinations Syndicate
International Examinations

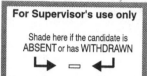
Examination Details	9999/01	99/D99
Examination Title	First Certificate in English	
Centre/Candidate No.	AA999/9999	
Candidate Name	A.N. EXAMPLE	

• Sign here if the details above are correct

• Tell the Supervisor now if the details above
are not correct

Candidate Answer Sheet: FCE Paper 1 Reading

Use a pencil

Mark ONE letter for each question.

For example, if you think **B** is the right answer to the question, mark your answer sheet like this:

| 0 | A | B | C | D |

Change your answer like this:

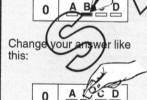

| 0 | A | | C | D |

1	A B C D E F G H I
2	A B C D E F G H I
3	A B C D E F G H I
4	A B C D E F G H I
5	A B C D E F G H I

6	A B C D E F G H I
7	A B C D E F G H I
8	A B C D E F G H I
9	A B C D E F G H I
10	A B C D E F G H I
11	A B C D E F G H I
12	A B C D E F G H I
13	A B C D E F G H I
14	A B C D E F G H I
15	A B C D E F G H I
16	A B C D E F G H I
17	A B C D E F G H I
18	A B C D E F G H I
19	A B C D E F G H I
20	A B C D E F G H I

21	A B C D E F G H I
22	A B C D E F G H I
23	A B C D E F G H I
24	A B C D E F G H I
25	A B C D E F G H I
26	A B C D E F G H I
27	A B C D E F G H I
28	A B C D E F G H I
29	A B C D E F G H I
30	A B C D E F G H I
31	A B C D E F G H I
32	A B C D E F G H I
33	A B C D E F G H I
34	A B C D E F G H I
35	A B C D E F G H I

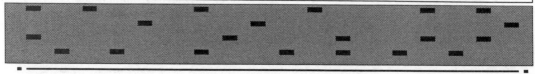

CAMBRIDGE
EXAMINATIONS, CERTIFICATES AND DIPLOMAS
ENGLISH AS A FOREIGN LANGUAGE

University of Cambridge
Local Examinations Syndicate
International   Examinations

Examination Details   9999/03   99/D99

Examination Title   First Certificate in English

Centre/Candidate No.   AA999/9999

Candidate Name   A.N. EXAMPLE

• Sign here if the details above are correct

• Tell the Supervisor now if the details above
  are not correct

Candidate Answer Sheet: FCE Paper 3 Use of English

Use a pencil

For **Part 1**: Mark ONE letter for each question.

For example, if you think **C** is the
right answer to the question,
mark your answer sheet like this:

| 0 | A̲ B̲ C̲ D̲ |

For **Parts 2, 3, 4** and **5**: Write your
answers in the spaces next to the
numbers like this:

| 0 | *example* |

Part 1					Part 2		Do not write here
1	A̲	B̲	C̲	D̲	16		▭ 16 ▭
2	A̲	B̲	C̲	D̲	17		▭ 17 ▭
3	A̲	B̲	C̲	D̲	18		▭ 18 ▭
4	A̲	B̲	C̲	D̲	19		▭ 19 ▭
5	A̲	B̲	C̲	D̲	20		▭ 20 ▭
6	A̲	B̲	C̲	D̲	21		▭ 21 ▭
7	A̲	B̲	C̲	D̲	22		▭ 22 ▭
8	A̲	B̲	C̲	D̲	23		▭ 23 ▭
9	A̲	B̲	C̲	D̲	24		▭ 24 ▭
10	A̲	B̲	C̲	D̲	25		▭ 25 ▭
11	A̲	B̲	C̲	D̲	26		▭ 26 ▭
12	A̲	B̲	C̲	D̲	27		▭ 27 ▭
13	A̲	B̲	C̲	D̲	28		▭ 28 ▭
14	A̲	B̲	C̲	D̲	29		▭ 29 ▭
15	A̲	B̲	C̲	D̲	30		▭ 30 ▭

Turn
over
for
Parts
3 - 5
→

Part 3		Do not write here		
31		31 0	1	2
32		32 0	1	2
33		33 0	1	2
34		34 0	1	2
35		35 0	1	2
36		36 0	1	2
37		37 0	1	2
38		38 0	1	2
39		39 0	1	2
40		40 0	1	2

Part 4		Do not write here	
41		41	
42		42	
43		43	
44		44	
45		45	
46		46	
47		47	
48		48	
49		49	
50		50	
51		51	
52		52	
53		53	
54		54	
55		55	

Part 5		Do not write here	
56		56	
57		57	
58		58	
59		59	
60		60	
61		61	
62		62	
63		63	
64		64	
65		65	

SAMPLE

183

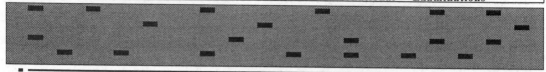

CAMBRIDGE
EXAMINATIONS, CERTIFICATES AND DIPLOMAS
ENGLISH AS A FOREIGN LANGUAGE

University of Cambridge
Local Examinations Syndicate
International   Examinations

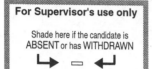

For Supervisor's use only

Shade here if the candidate is
ABSENT or has WITHDRAWN

➡ ▭ ⬅

☒

Examination Details	9999/04
Examination Title	First Certificate in English
Centre/Candidate No.	AA999/9999
Candidate Name	A.N. EXAMPLE

99/D99

• Sign here if the details above are correct

• Tell the Supervisor now if the details above
  are not correct

Candidate Answer Sheet: FCE Paper 4 Listening

Mark test version below

A	B	C	D	E
▭	▭	▭	▭	▭

Use a pencil

For **Parts 1** and **3**:
Mark ONE letter for
each question.

For example, if you
think **B** is the right
answer to the
question, mark your
answer sheet like this:

0	A	B	C
	▭	▬	▭

For **Parts 2** and **4**:
Write your answers in
the spaces next to the
numbers like this:

0	*example*

Part 1

1	A	B	C
2	A	B	C
3	A	B	C
4	A	B	C
5	A	B	C
6	A	B	C
7	A	B	C
8	A	B	C

Part 2 | Do not write here
9	9
10	10
11	11
12	12
13	13
14	14
15	15
16	16
17	17
18	18

Part 3

19	A	B	C	D	E	F
20	A	B	C	D	E	F
21	A	B	C	D	E	F
22	A	B	C	D	E	F
23	A	B	C	D	E	F

Part 4 | Do not write here
24	24
25	25
26	26
27	27
28	28
29	29
30	30

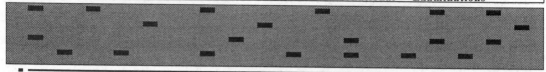

184